Sacred Shanghai
Liz Hingley

By ritual, Heaven and Earth harmoniously combine.
Xunzi (3rd century BC Chinese philosopher)

GOST

致谢

许多不同世界的碰撞成就了这部作品，我对这种碰撞的产生感到十分欣喜。我想向我在上海遇见的人和地方致以永恒的感谢，以下的致谢是我的衷心表达。这些记忆不断地给我带来惊喜、灵感，并用不绝的惊讶与赞叹填充着我。

我于2013年搬到上海，与复旦大学哲学学院徐光启—利玛窦文明对话研究中心的 Benoît Vermander 教授和上海社会科学院的张靓组成了一个小团队。我们希望针对中国某一城市的宗教实践做一次彻底调查，这是前所未有的。我们的合作非常愉快。

这项深入的调查持续了五年，并以2018年华盛顿大学出版社出版的一本专著结束。我曾经在上海社会科学院担任访问学者，而这项工作同样受益于徐光启—利玛窦文明对话研究中心、亚洲研究中心和上海社会科学院的慷慨支持。

Claire Dwyer 教授、施翰涛、Sirkka Lisa-Konttinen、Linda Woodhead 教授、David Jasper 教授、Karen Smith (凯伦) 和 Ian Johnson (张彦) 帮助我发现这项实践的价值，我衷心感谢你们的热情、参与和付出。

在上海的日子里，我从很多人身上汲取了创作能量和友谊。我尤其感谢 Charlotte Middlehurst (夏洛婷)、Rachel Marsden (马十灯)、张婷、陈航峰、Francesca Girelli (葛拂兰)、王慧英、Carol Allen- Storey、Alys Tomlinson、Eike Stratmann、Yoshinori Kawamura、Nora Wuttke、伊萝、和季怡雯。

我要感谢 Max Duncan (马昕默)、Felicity Bryan、Francis Henley Lock、Rob、Bernadette、Helen 和 Catherine Hingley – 是你们的倾听、言语和爱使我坚持下去。

感谢来自 GOST 的每一个人，你们给予我对这部作品全新的认知，并帮我用它创造了美好。

最后，我感激每一个愿意接受拍摄的受访者。谢谢你们分享你们的情感。

Acknowledgements

A lot of worlds collided in the making of this work, and I am so glad they did. These acknowledgements are a heartfelt expression of eternal thanks to the people and places I encountered in Shanghai. These memories continue to surprise, inspire and fill me with wonder.

I moved to Shanghai in 2013 to form a small team with Professor Benoît Vermander of the Xu-Ricci Dialogue Institute at Fudan University and Liang Zhang of the Shanghai Academy of Social Sciences. We aimed to make the first thorough investigation of religious practice in a Chinese city. Our collaboration was extraordinary.

This intensive mission took us five years and culminated in a monograph published by Washington University Press in 2018. The project was made possible through the generous support of Xu-Ricci Dialogue Institute, Asia Centre and the Shanghai Academy of Social Sciences, where I was a visiting scholar.

Professor Claire Dwyer, Shi Hantao, Sirkka Lisa-Konttinen, Professor Linda Woodhead, Professor David Jasper, Karen Smith and Ian Johnson helped me see the value of my practice—thank you for your enthusiasm, commitment and input.

My time in Shanghai was fuelled by the creative energy and friendship of Charlotte Middlehurst, Rachel Marsden, Ting Zhang, Chen Hangfeng, Carol Allen-Storey, Alys Tomlinson, Francesca Girelli, Jasmin Ong, Eike Stratmann, Yoshinori Kawamura, Nora Wuttke, Mose Yilou and Ji Yiwen among many others.

Max Duncan, Felicity Bryan, Francis Henley Lock, Rob, Bernadette, Helen and Catherine Hingley—your ears, words and love kept me afloat.

Thank you to the exceptional GOST team—you gave me renewed belief in this work and helped make something so beautiful with it!

Lastly, I am indebted to everyone who agreed to be photographed. Thank you for sharing your passions.

与信仰的亲密关系
Ian Johnson

仅仅几十年前，中国的生活仍以村庄为基础，人们在有着嘈杂音乐、沸腾的香炉和炫目表演的团体仪式中寻找意义，试图取悦、哄骗或批评他们的神灵。这类古老的宗教仍然存在，但信仰在中国却变得愈发安静、私人和静默，且十分秘密。它仍然充满了喜悦和活力，但在那些主导着中国人生活的庞大后资本主义城市里，个体们正为了寻找意义而挣扎其中。

上海是中国最大最都市化的城市。生活在那儿的那些年里，Liz Hingley 拉开一副窗帘，其后遮蔽的是一个很多人难以触碰的世界。她的图片点亮了一个与过去村庄生活相去甚远的中国：一个交织着摩天大楼和国际化商业、新颖的生活方式和理念、新技术和文化信仰汇集的城市。简单地说，这是中国未来的缩影。

几十年前，这般景象可能难以想象。直到上世纪90年代以前，80%左右的中国人口仍生活在乡村，像上海这样的城市是个例外。当中国的经济腾飞给沿海地区带来就业，几百万人口开始向这些新兴都市迁移。他们当中很多只是短暂停留，但越来越多的人在为长远打算。90年代初开始，这种趋势开始加速，许多内陆城市也纷纷起跑。乡村空了，一大部分的中国人口移居到城镇地带，推动了生活方式和处世思考的变化。

如今，人们对个体的关注超越了其社群属性，信仰也因此变得更像是个人主义的表达。抛开出生地的约束，中国新一代的城市居民创造了新的身份认同，并为自己找到了真实的信仰。

The Intimacy of Faith
Ian Johnson

Just a few decades ago, life in China was based in villages, where people found meaning in raucous communal ceremonies of loud music, billowing pots of incense and colourful performances to please, cajole, or criticise their gods. Some of that old-style religion still exists, but faith in China now is increasingly quiet, personal, contemplative and most of all, private. It is still full of joy and exuberance, but also where individuals struggle to find meaning in the big, post-capitalist cities that now dominate Chinese life.

Through the years she spent living in Shanghai—China's largest and most cosmopolitan city—Liz Hingley has lifted a curtain on a world that for many, is hard to penetrate. Her images bring to light a China far from the village life of years past: a place of high-rises and globalized commerce, of new ways of living and new beliefs, of new technologies and a convergence among faiths and cultures—in short, a microcosm of China's future.

Just a few decades ago, this landscape would have been hard to imagine. Up until the 1990s, about 80 percent of the Chinese population lived in villages and cities like Shanghai were the exception. As China's economic boom created jobs for people in coastal areas, millions began to move to these boomtowns, many for short stays, but increasingly, for the long haul. Since the early 90s the pace has picked up, with scores of cities in China's interior still growing rapidly as well. As villages empty out, a majority of the Chinese population is moving to urban areas, helping to

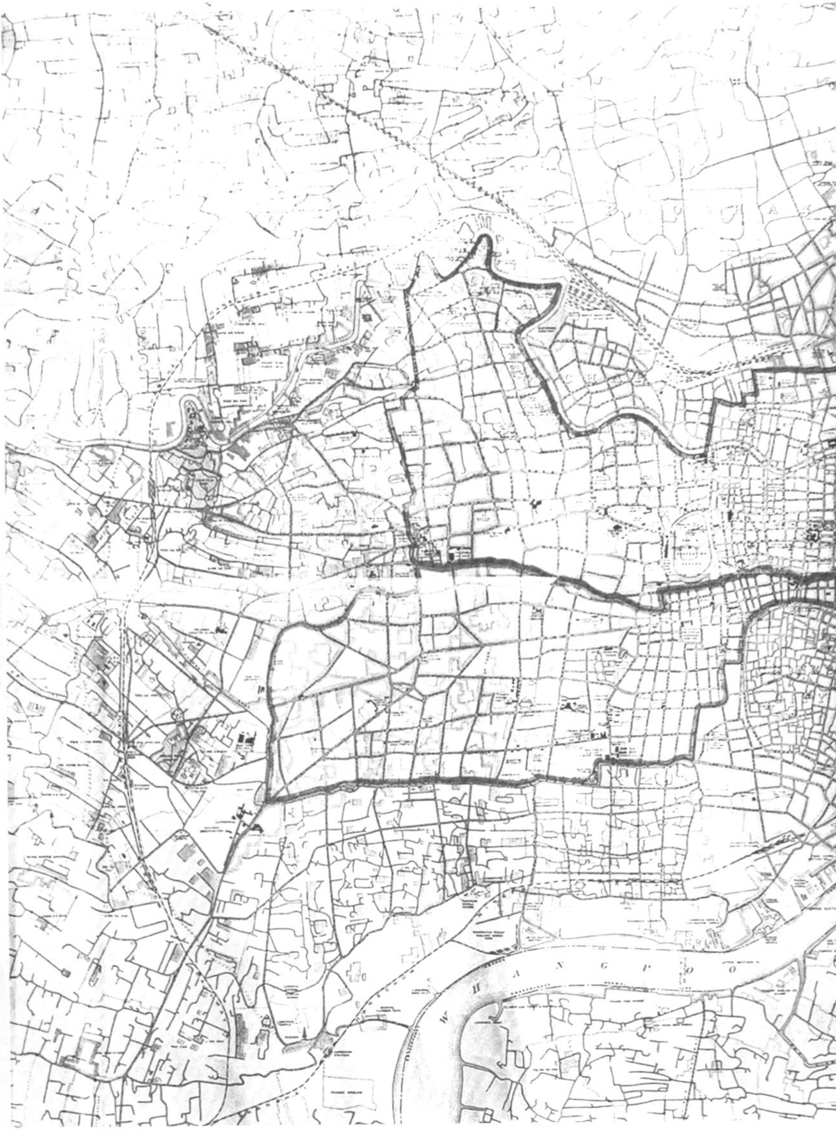
W H A N G P O O

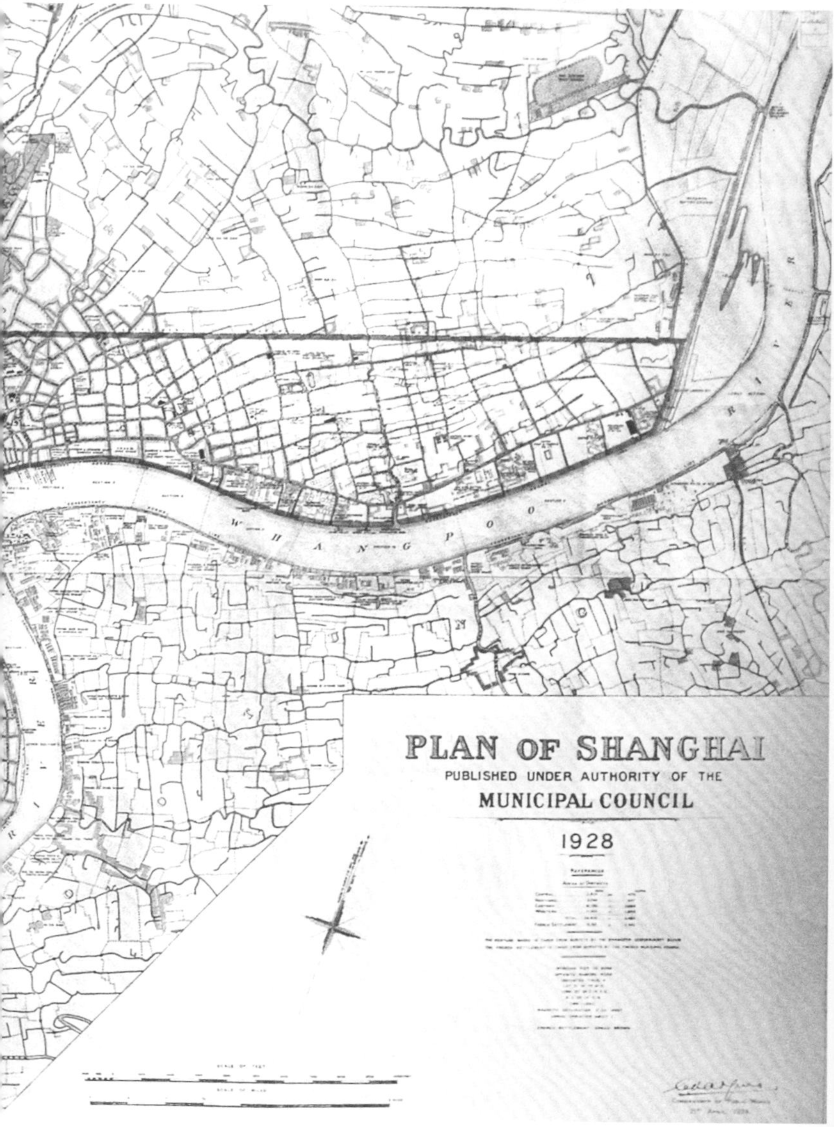
W H A N G P O O
R I V E R
PLAN OF SHANGHAI
PUBLISHED UNDER AUTHORITY OF THE
MUNICIPAL COUNCIL
1928

对于很多中国人来说，关于如何塑造个人宗教、信仰和信念系统，一个拥有无限可能的世界正在打开。这种新的未知助推了中国那些非传统宗教，尤其是基督教。基督教在当今中国成长最为迅速，部分原因是它能在中国的大城市中找到落脚点。

但这并不意味着社群已不再重要。对很多人来说，城市生活是让人困惑的。人们在这种社会空间中感到疑惑，他们不再熟悉自己的邻居，传统的价值观也变得无足轻重，只有钱在主宰一切。宗教使上海这样的城市不那么难以忍受。在教堂、寺庙或清真寺里，城市居民们找到了志同道合的社团，在一个需要路标引导的社会中给他们带来支持。

在这个新世界里，人们选择他们自己的宗教领袖，这当中的许多甚至与官方认可的宗教毫不相关。衣食无忧的城里人和活佛们一起斋戒，或在漆黑的洞穴中学习冥想；他们涉猎神秘学，或重新体验包含强烈精神象征的传统武术。他们混合并实验着 – 总而言之，他们表现地像西方和其他很多国家的人那样，感受着传统信仰的彼此挤压、交汇、融合。

科技推动了一些这样的转变。在中国，手机和平板电脑无处不在，社交媒体平台让改变的速度难以追赶。这种状况使得人们能绕过既有的宗教组织，围绕一些圣贤之人组成社团。信徒们偶尔在仪式上相聚，但更多通过信息、视频和发布文章保持日常联系，以传达何时、何地、如何祷告。不出意外地，这种生活更加向内聚焦，人们独自面对着自己的信仰。这些通常是人们独自沉思、爱恋、大笑或独处的时刻。有时它们在现代城市

change ways of life and ways of thinking about their place in the universe.

Today, people are less defined by their community than by their personal concerns, making faith more of an expression of individualism. Freed from being defined by where they were born, China's new urbanites have created new identities, discovering for themselves what they truly believe.

For many Chinese, a world of possibilities for how to shape one's religion, faith, and belief system is now opening. This new potential is helping boost non-traditional religions in China—in particular Christianity—now China's fastest-growing faith, in part because it seems better able to find a foothold in the country's new megacities.

That's not to say community doesn't matter. For many, city life is confusing. People are bewildered by a social space where they no longer know their neighbours and where traditional values count for little—money seems to be all that matters. Religions help take the edge off the harshness of cities like Shanghai. In churches, temples, or mosques, city dwellers find ready-made communities of like-minded people—a support group for a society in need of guideposts.

In this new world, people choose their own gurus, many of them not affiliated with any of the officially sanctioned religions. Well-off urban Chinese go on fasting cures with Tibetan Rinpoches or learn to meditate in pitch-black caves; they dabble in the occult, or rediscover traditional martial arts—which often have a strong spiritual component. They mix and experiment—in short, they behave like people in many other countries, including the West, where traditional

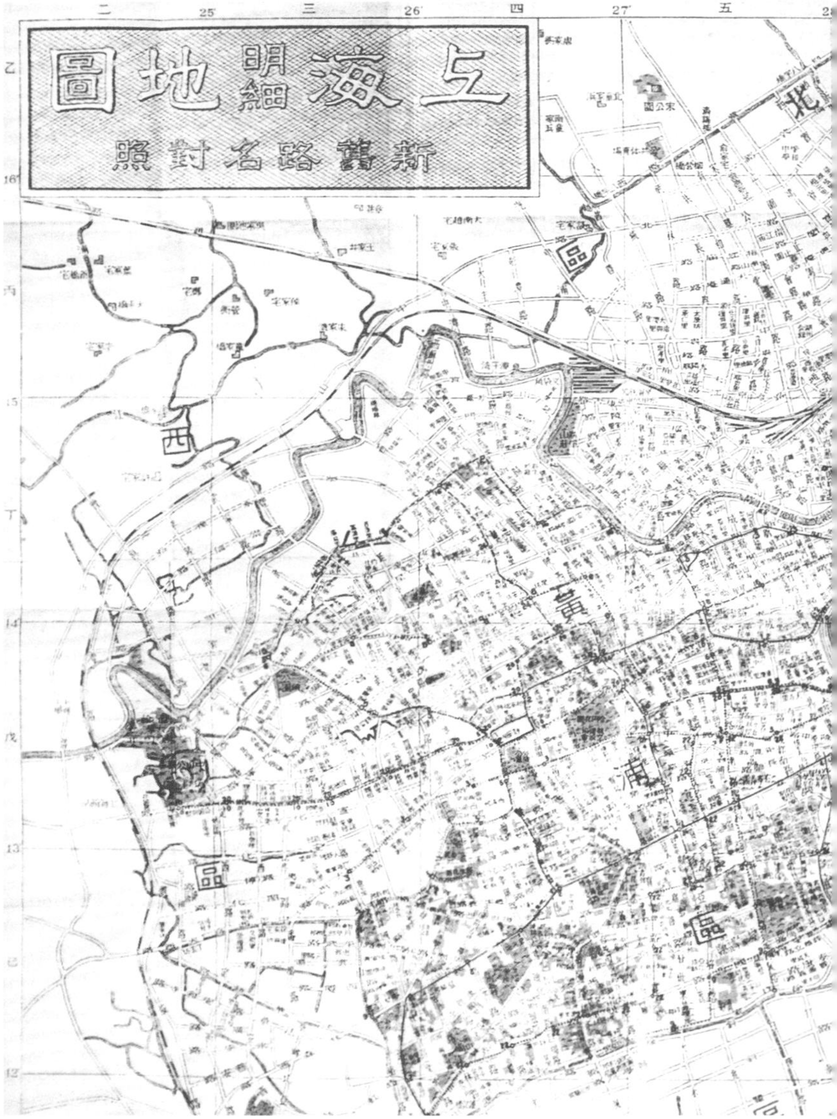
上海明細地圖
新舊路名對照

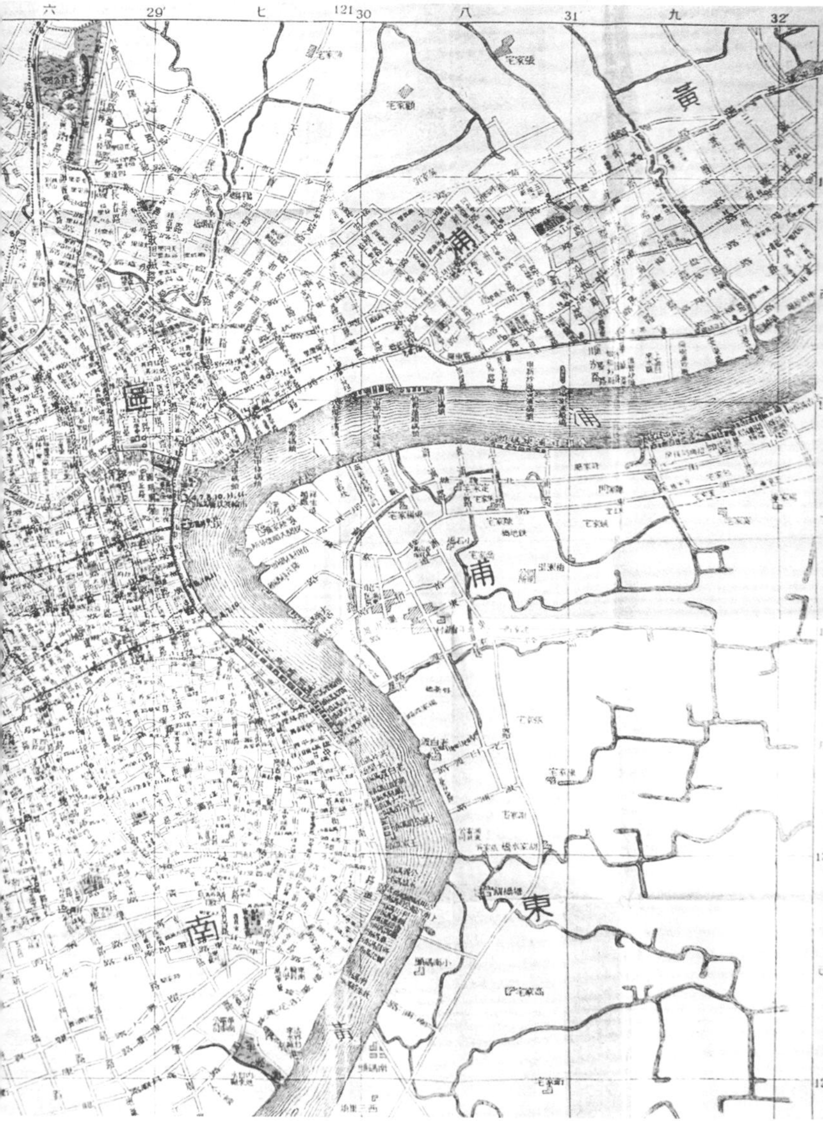

六
29′
七
121 30
八
31′
九
32′
16
丙
15
丁
14
戊
13
己
12′
黄
浦
區
浦
浦
東
南

常见的摩天大楼和公寓楼里悄然发生，有时也存在于那些点缀城市生活的旧式习俗中：比如一顿传统的新年晚餐，为逝者燃烧纸房子、纸车和纸钱的坚持，以及在婚礼、孩子出世时和葬礼上的喧嚣乐队。

正因为像上海这样的大型都市如此多样化，外国人也成为其文化景观的一个组成。作为一个贸易大国，几百万的外国人将全新的、异国的信仰带到这里。虽然追随这些外国信仰体系不被法律允许，许多中国人还是尝试接触巴哈教、俄罗斯东正教、或模仿着西方对藏传佛教的着迷。

佛教也以其他的方式在不断拓宽。有一定经济能力的中国人去国外旅行并发现东南亚和东亚的佛教与自己的信仰不同，因此丰富了他们的宗教生活。在中国看见泰国佛龛并不是什么稀奇的事情。

文化的交汇在这个新的宗教世界中有着重要作用。宗教并没有融合成一种单一信仰，但交汇的部分相当明显。过去，大多数中国人只与一种信仰的一小部分有交集，比如一个本地神灵或是地区道教或佛教的分支；如今人们面前则是许多不同信仰紧挨着彼此。

在中国，不仅神灵们无处不在，国家机器也是。警察对信徒的压制或对礼拜场所的毁坏在这个国家的不同角落仍会发生。但是，政府的角色不限于对加强控制的需求，它也希望参与其中。因此，博物馆中有被神化的革命领袖，赞颂民间英雄的大型公共艺术装置在各地的公园里也能看到。政府连传统中医里的精神元素也没有遗漏。近期有关中医的新法规正式承认了师承关系，这

faiths are bending, melding, and merging into one another.

Driving some of these changes is technology. Smartphones and tablets are ubiquitous in China, as are social media platforms that supercharge the pace of change. This allows people to bypass established religious organisations and form communities around sages and holy people. Believers meet up occasionally for ceremonies but mainly stay in daily touch through messages, videos, and articles that explain how, when and where to worship. Not surprisingly, this type of life is more inward-focused, where people face their belief on their own. These are often personal moments of contemplation, love, laughter, or alienation. Some of this takes place in the skyscrapers and apartment blocks that define modern Chinese cities, but also in the pockets of the past that still dot Chinese cities: a traditional New Year's dinner, the persistence of burning paper houses, cars, and money for the dead, or a rambunctious music group announcing a wedding, birth, or funeral.

Because greater metropolitan areas like Shanghai are so diverse, foreigners make up a portion of the cultural landscape. As a great trading nation, China is home to millions of non-Chinese who bring in new, 'exotic' faiths. Though not legally allowed to follow these foreign belief systems, many Chinese people experiment with Baha'i, Russian Orthodox Christianity, or emulate western fascination with Tibetan Buddhism.

Buddhism is broadening in other ways, too. With money to spend, Chinese are travelling abroad and discovering that Southeast and South Asian

毛主席语录

军民团结如一人，

试看天下谁能敌？

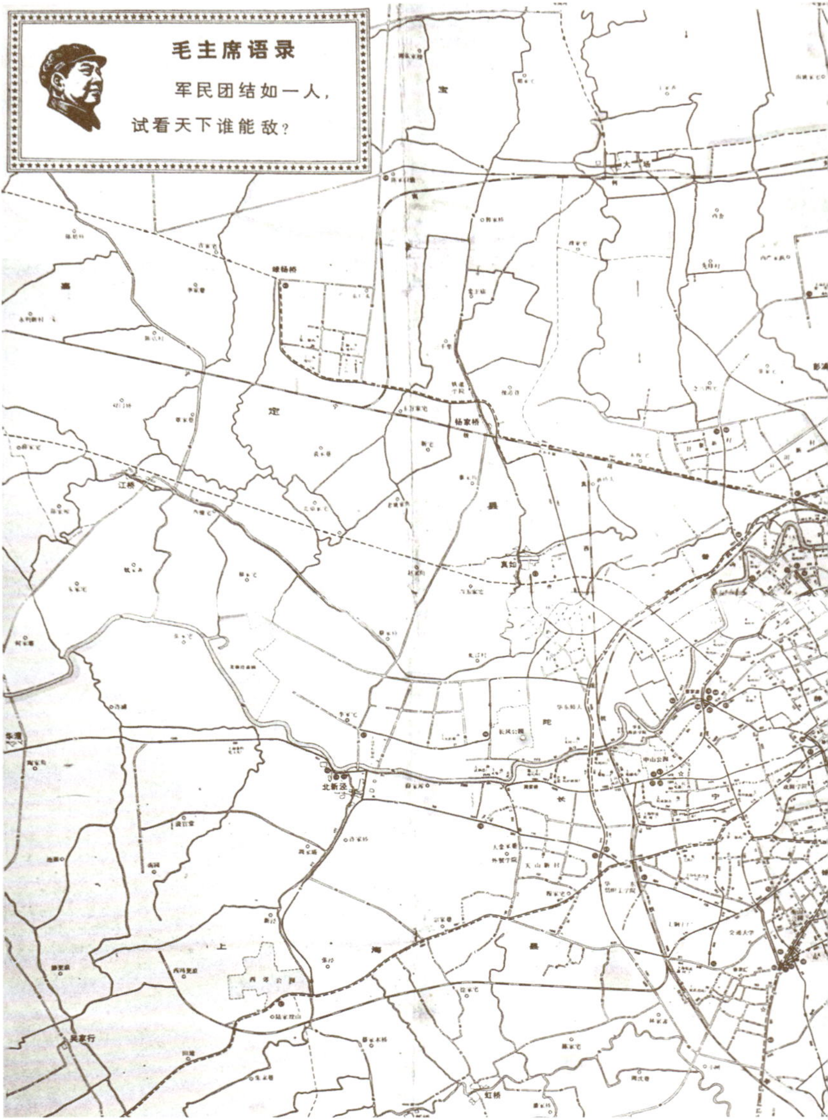

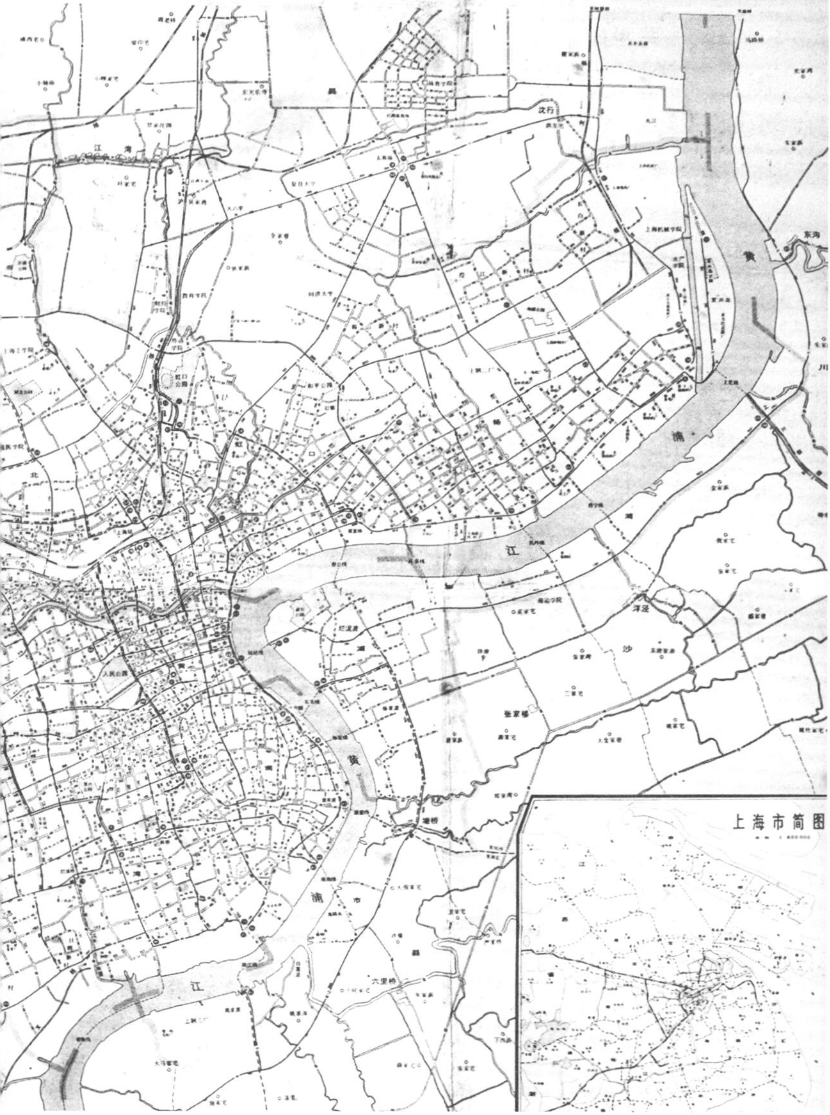
上海市简图
人民公园
虹口公园
复旦大学
同济大学
上海机械学院
东海
张家楼
洋泾
塘桥
六里桥

种关系往往包含着对老师的崇敬甚至接近膜拜。

信仰在中国也许脆弱，但它的重要性是不必怀疑的，尤其是在日渐异化的大城市中。它在人们心中的重要存在不可能彻底消除。超越经济和政治，这些点滴构成了中国的新内核。

Buddhism is different from theirs, yet can enrich their religious lives. It is not uncommon to see Thai Buddhist shrines in China.

Cultural convergence is a key part of this new religious world. Religions aren't all melding into one faith, but the overlaps are striking. In the past, most Chinese experienced one small part of one faith—maybe a local god or a regional variation of Taoism or Buddhism; now people are confronted with many faiths living cheek to jowl.

In China, the gods aren't just omnipresent, the state is too. Police crackdowns on believers or the demolition of places of worship in different parts of the country still occur. And yet the state's role is broader than simply its desire to enforce control; it seeks to be a player, too. And so deified revolutionary leaders are exhibited in museums and gargantuan public art projects meant to extol mythic heroes are seen in parks across the country. Even traditional medicine has a spiritual component that the state doesn't downplay. Recent new laws on Chinese medicine have given formal sanction to the master-disciple relationship, one that often includes reverence and near-worship of one's teacher.

Faith in China may be vulnerable, yet its unwavering importance—especially in alienating megacities—is beyond doubt. Its very presence in people's hearts makes it impossible to eradicate. More than economics or politics, it is these moments that are the new heart of China.

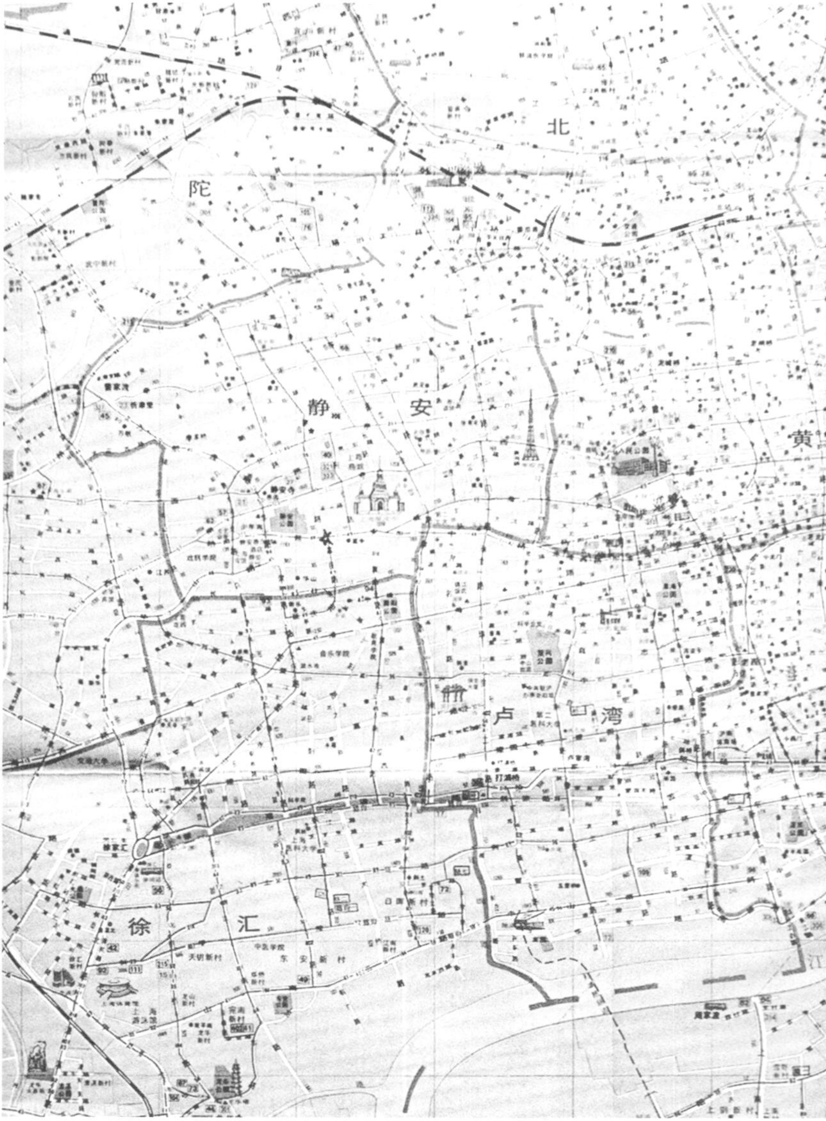

陀
北
静
安
黄
卢
湾
徐
汇

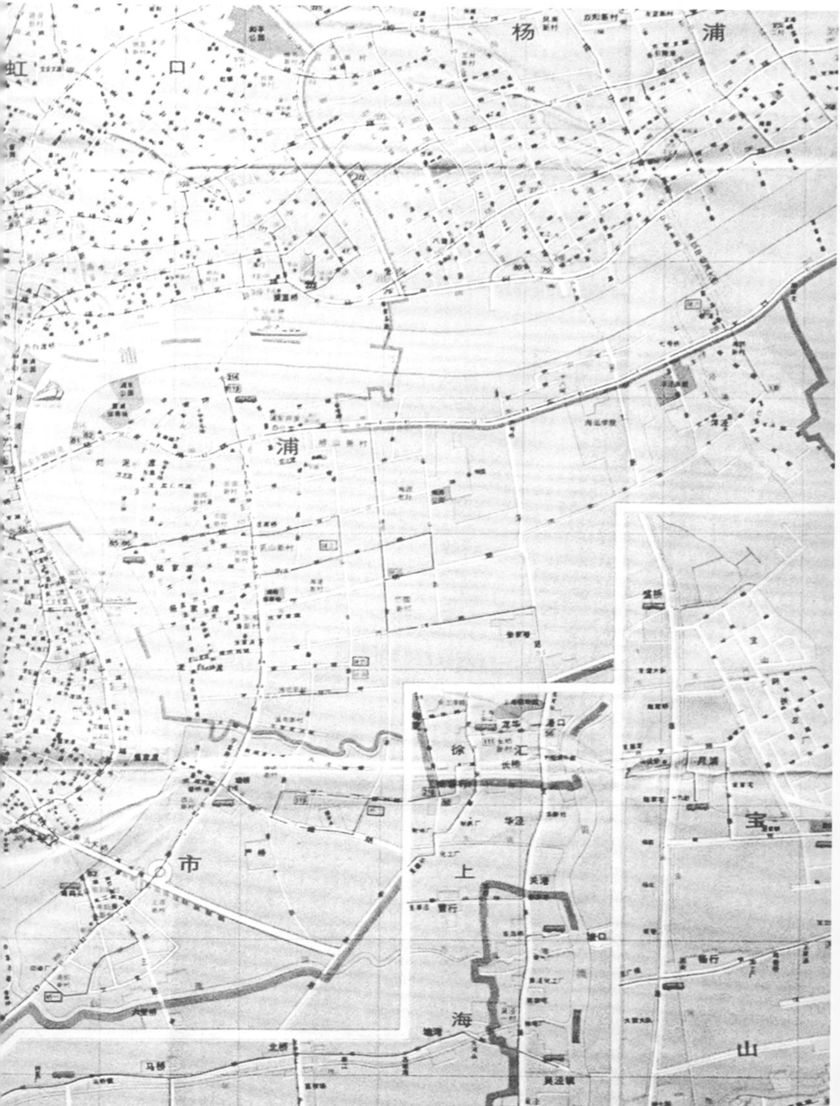
虹
口
杨
浦
浦
浦
徐
汇
宝
市
上
海
山

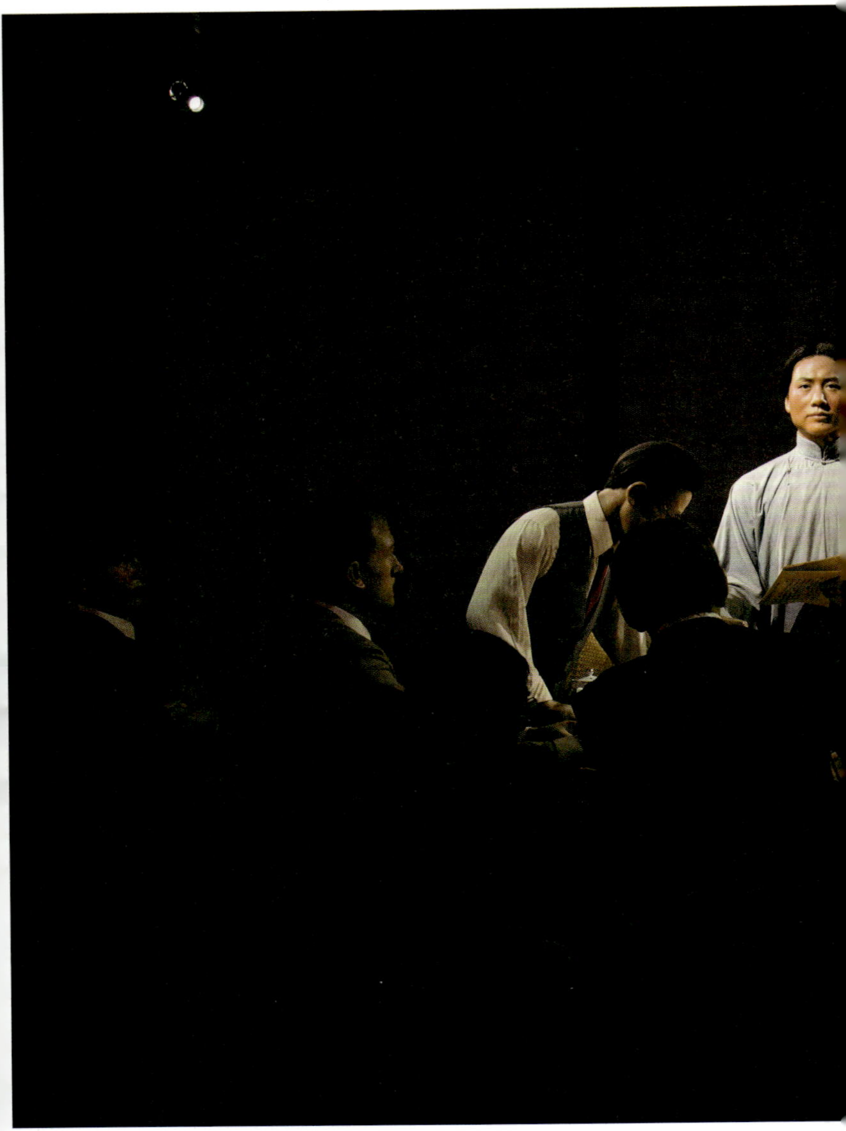

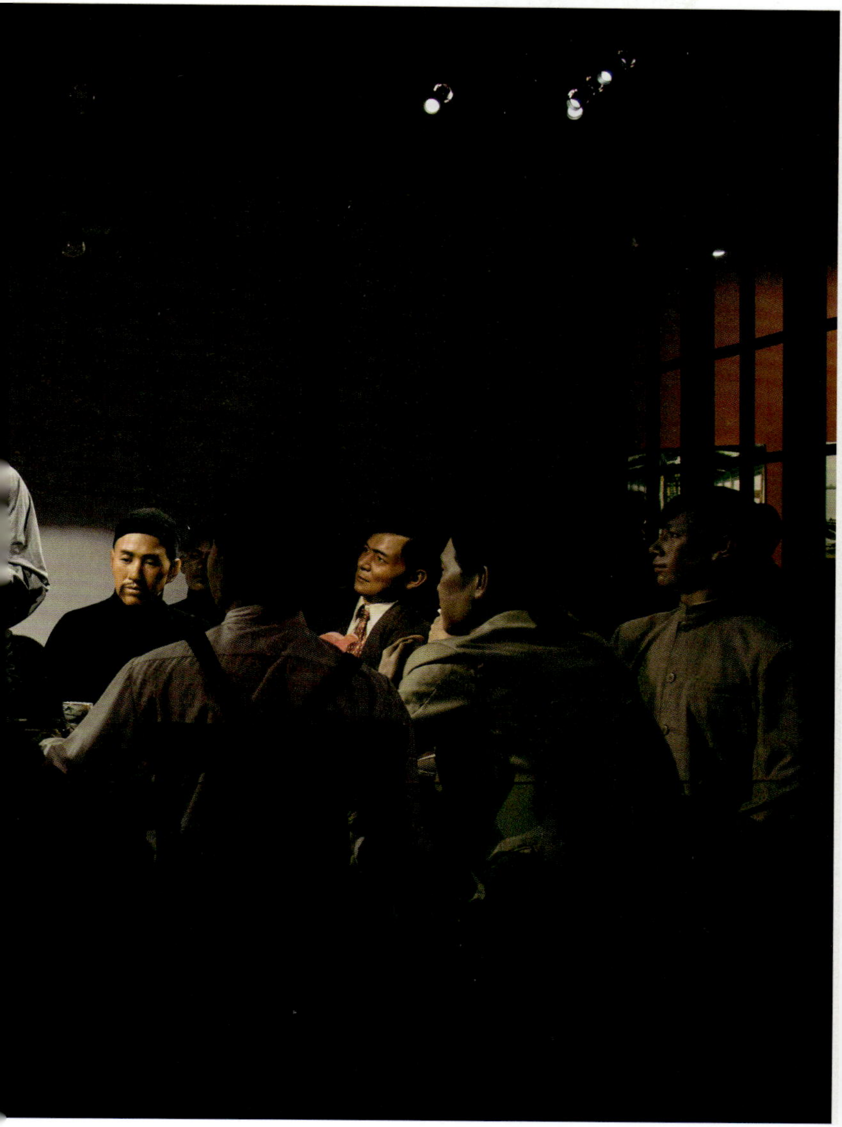

1

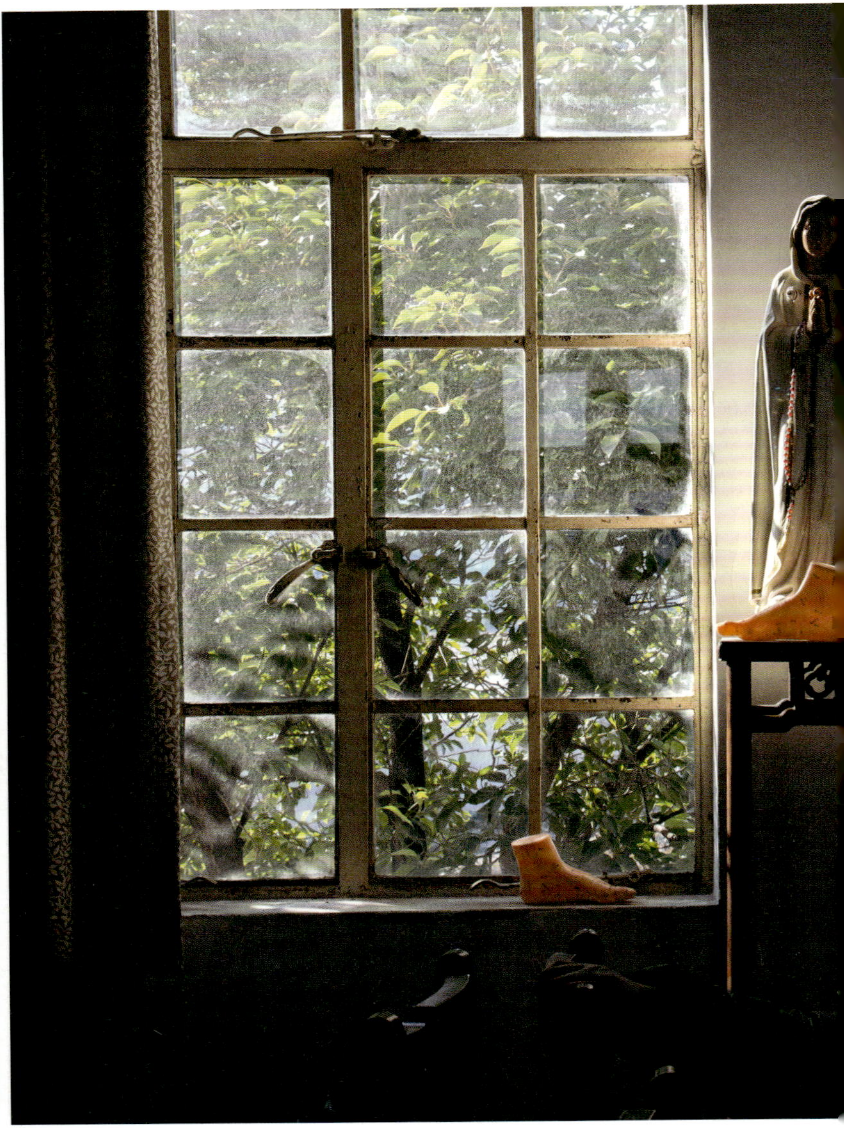

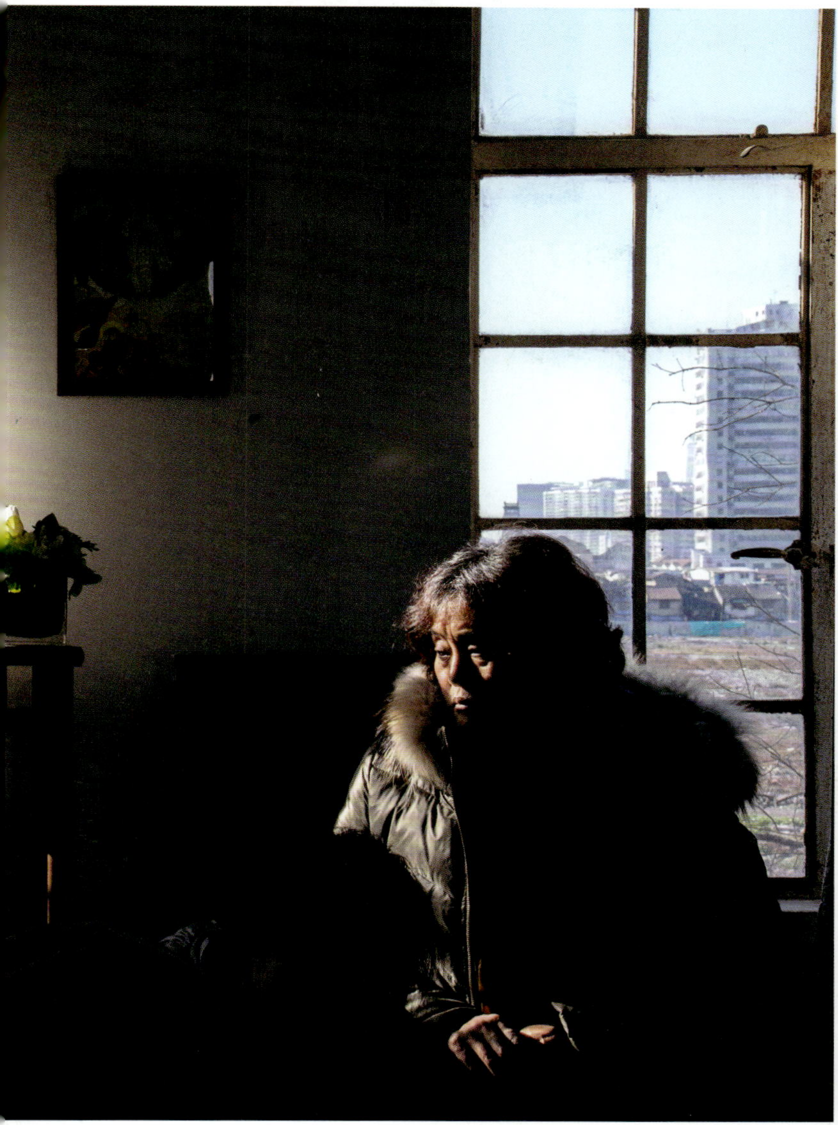

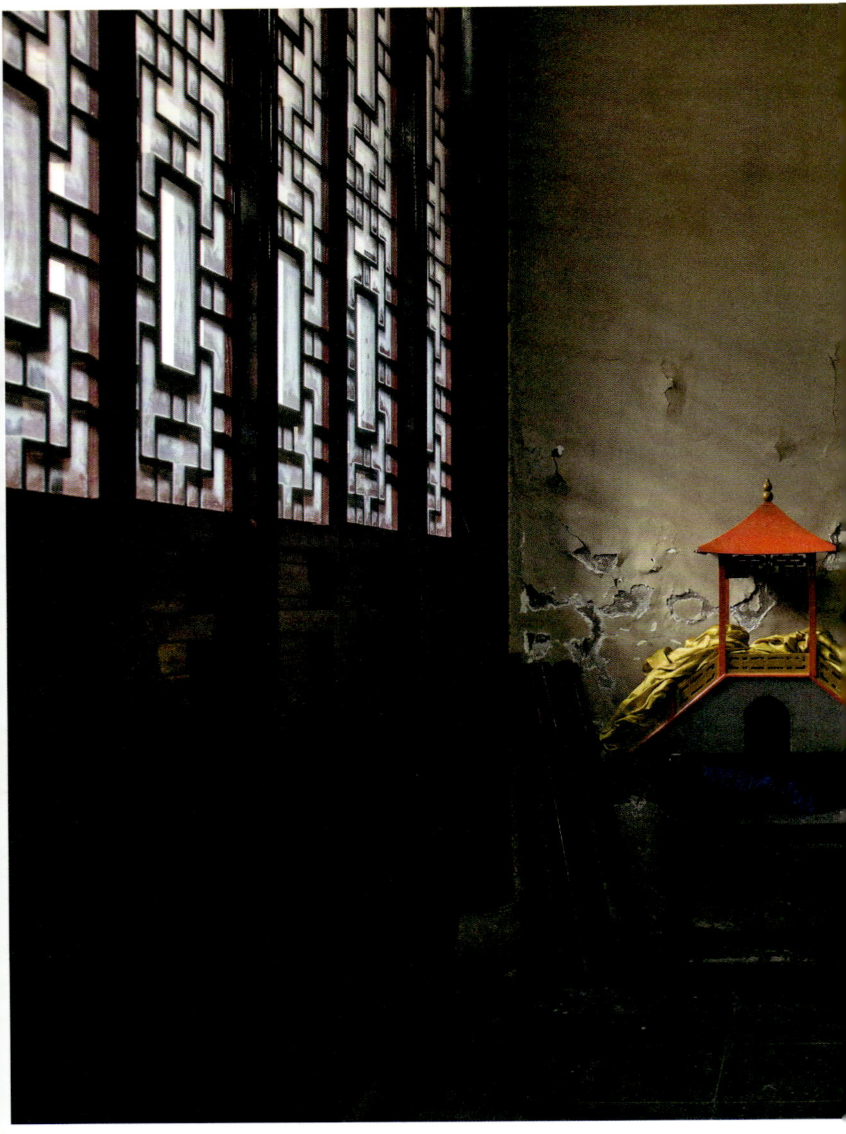

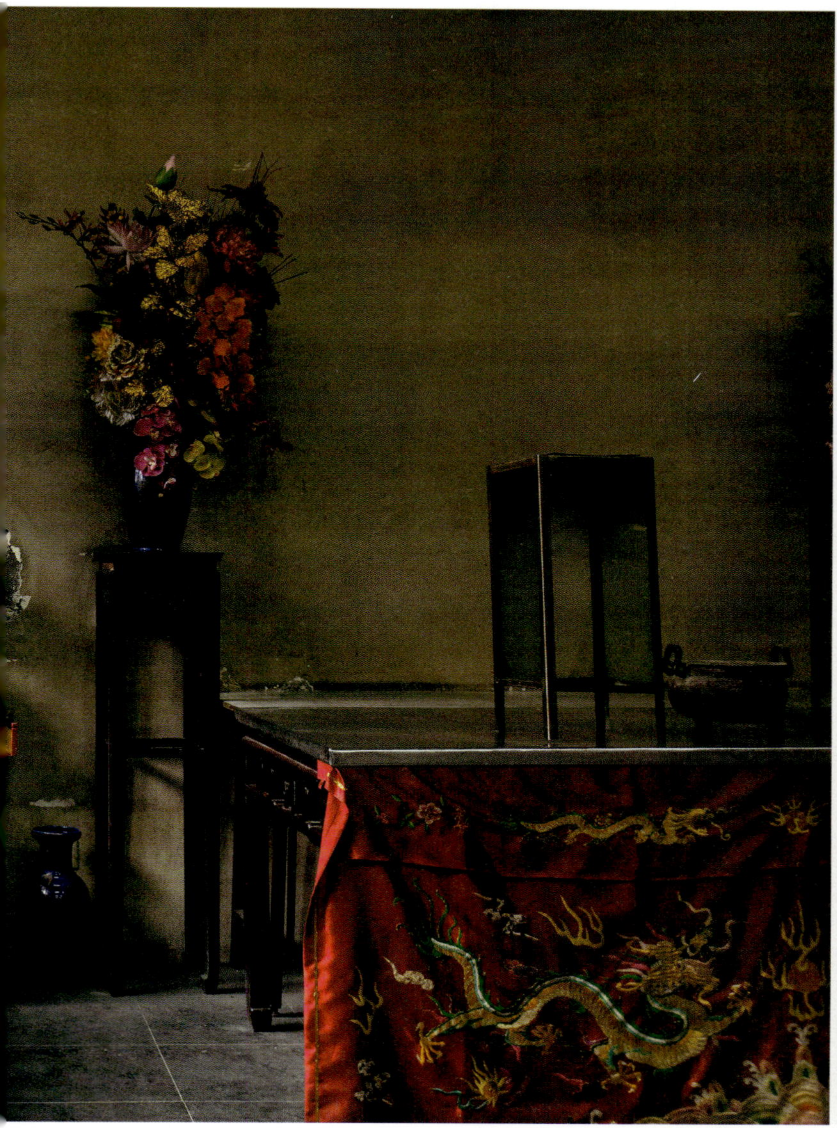

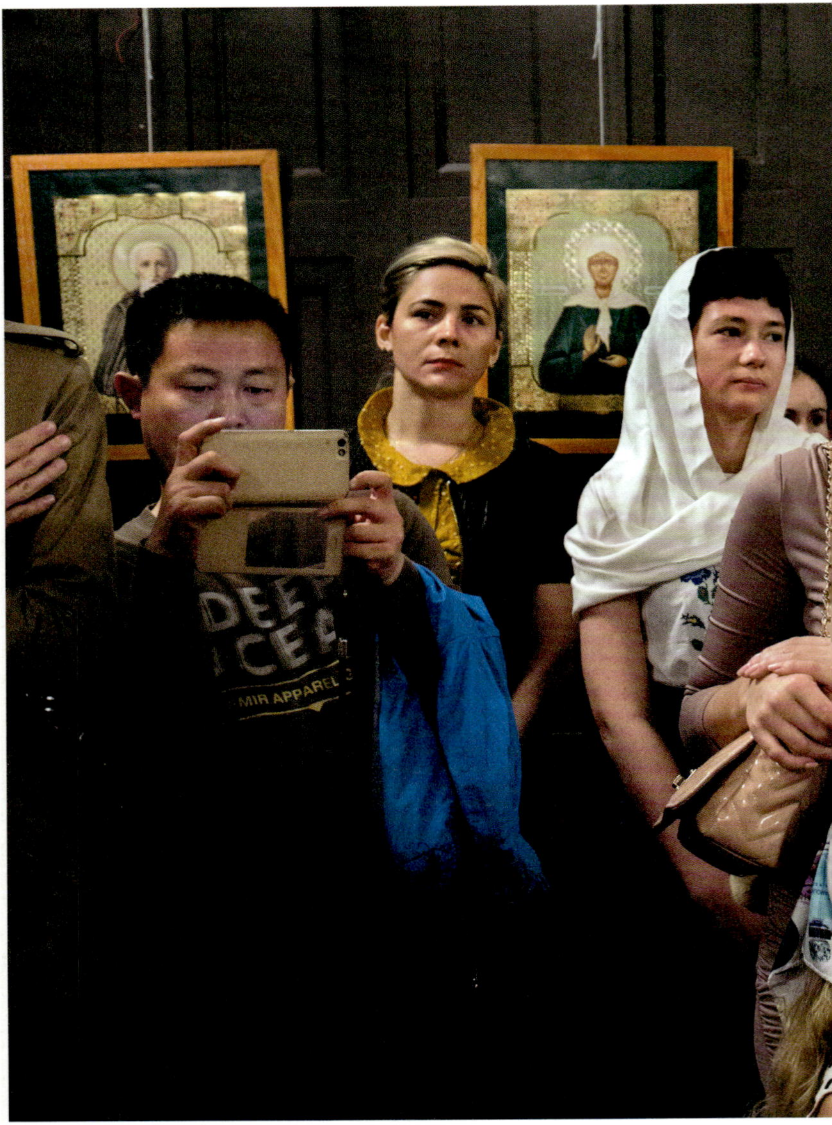
MIR APPAREL

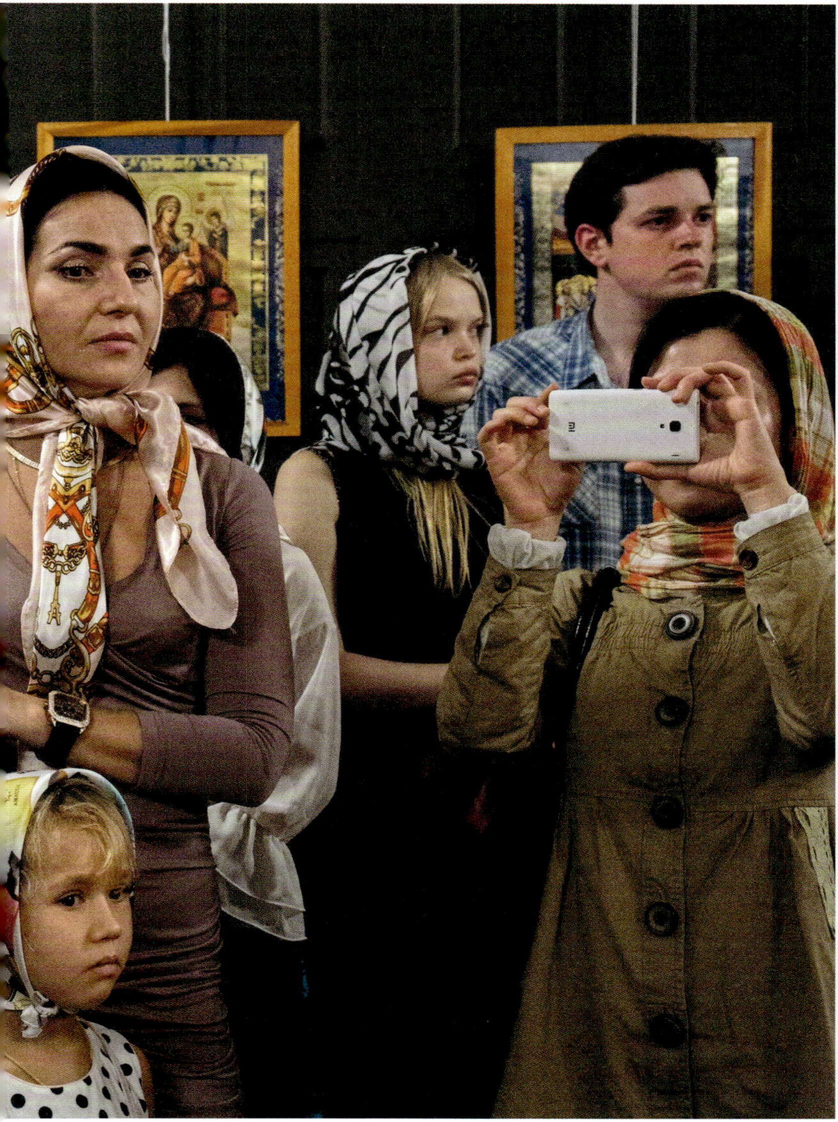

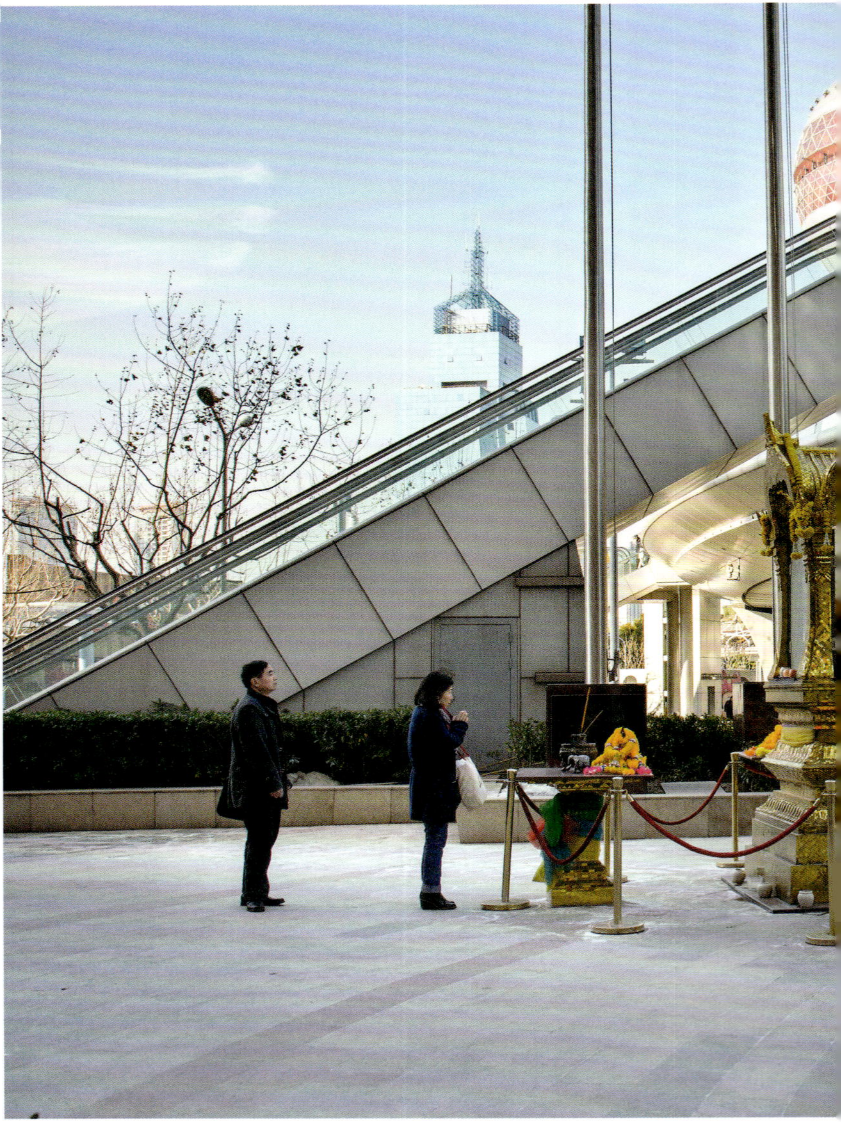

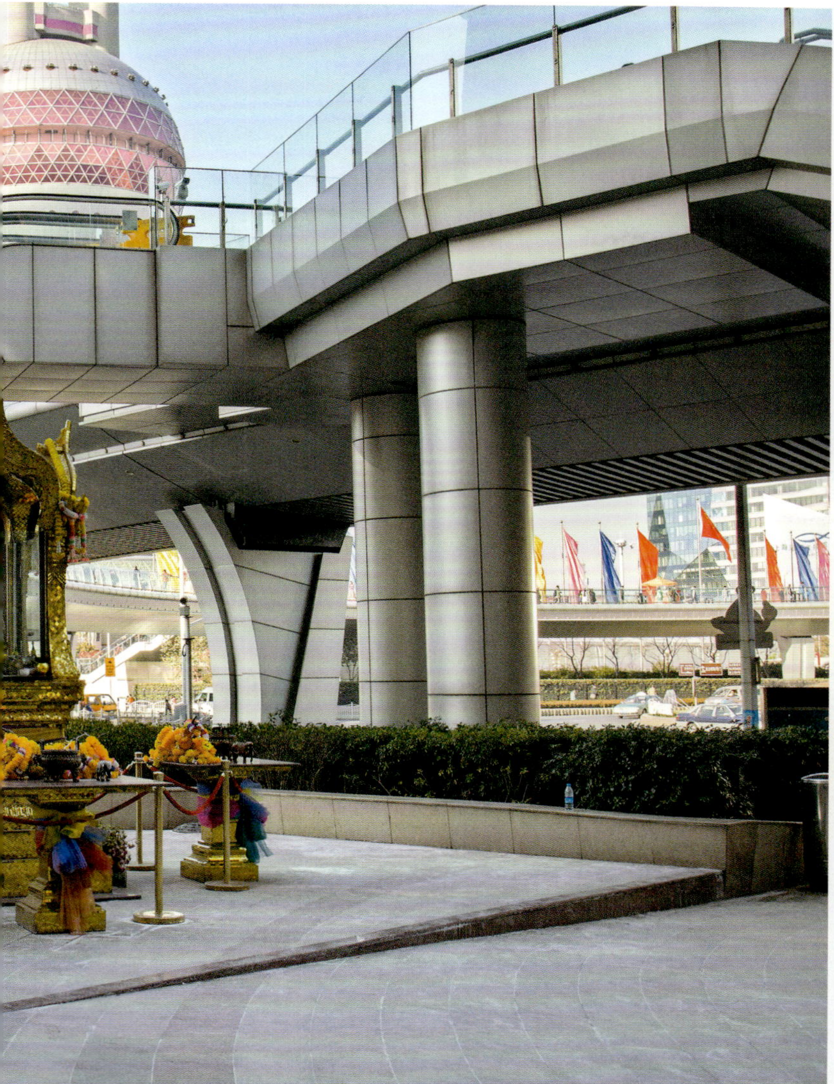

5

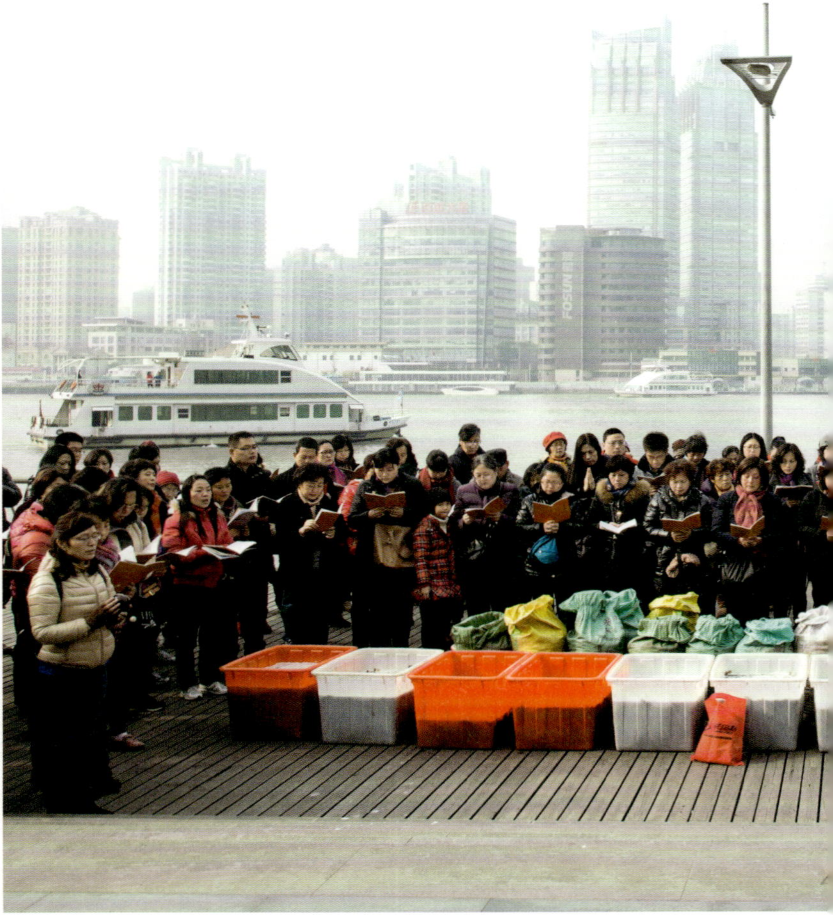
FOSUN

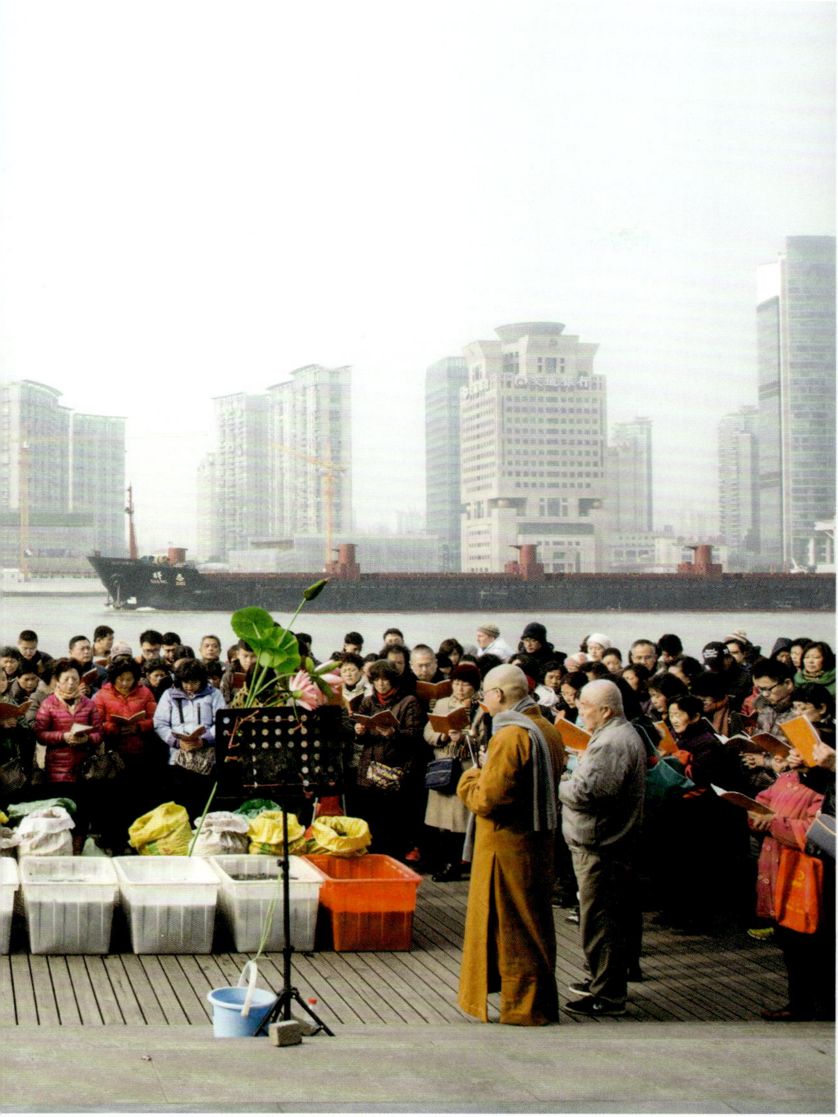

6

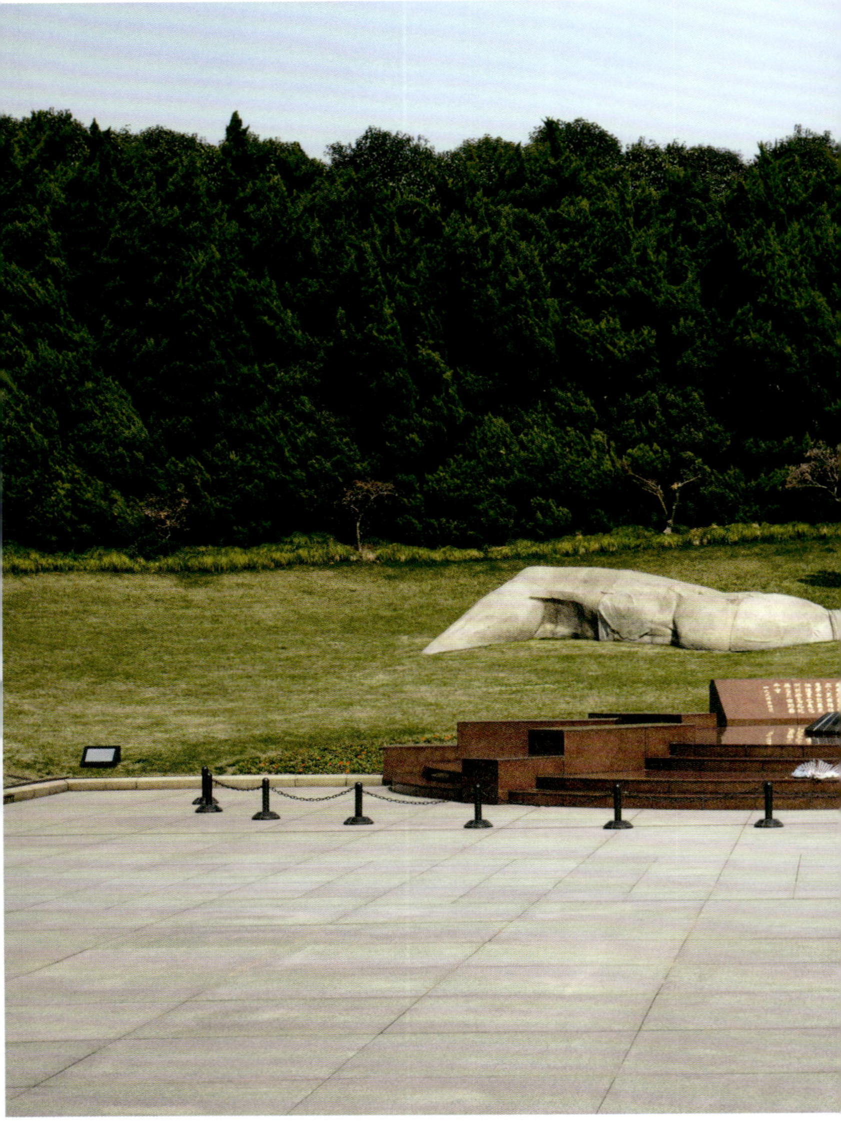

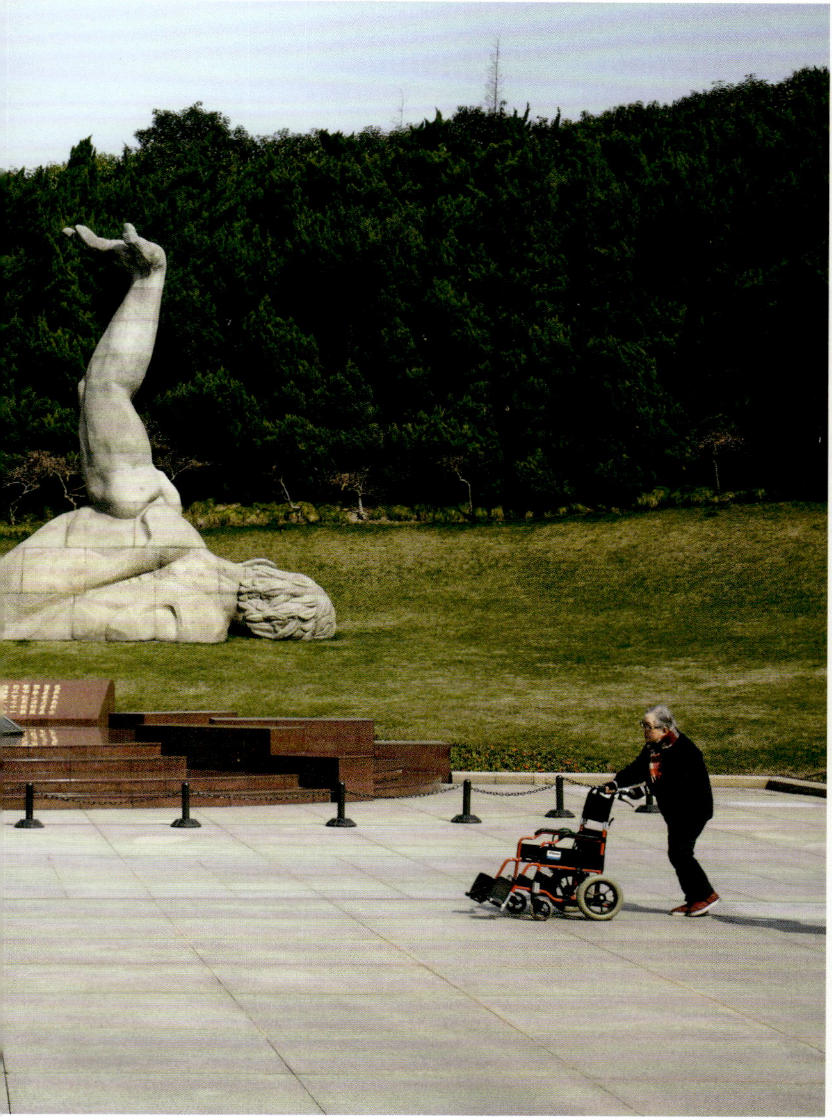

7

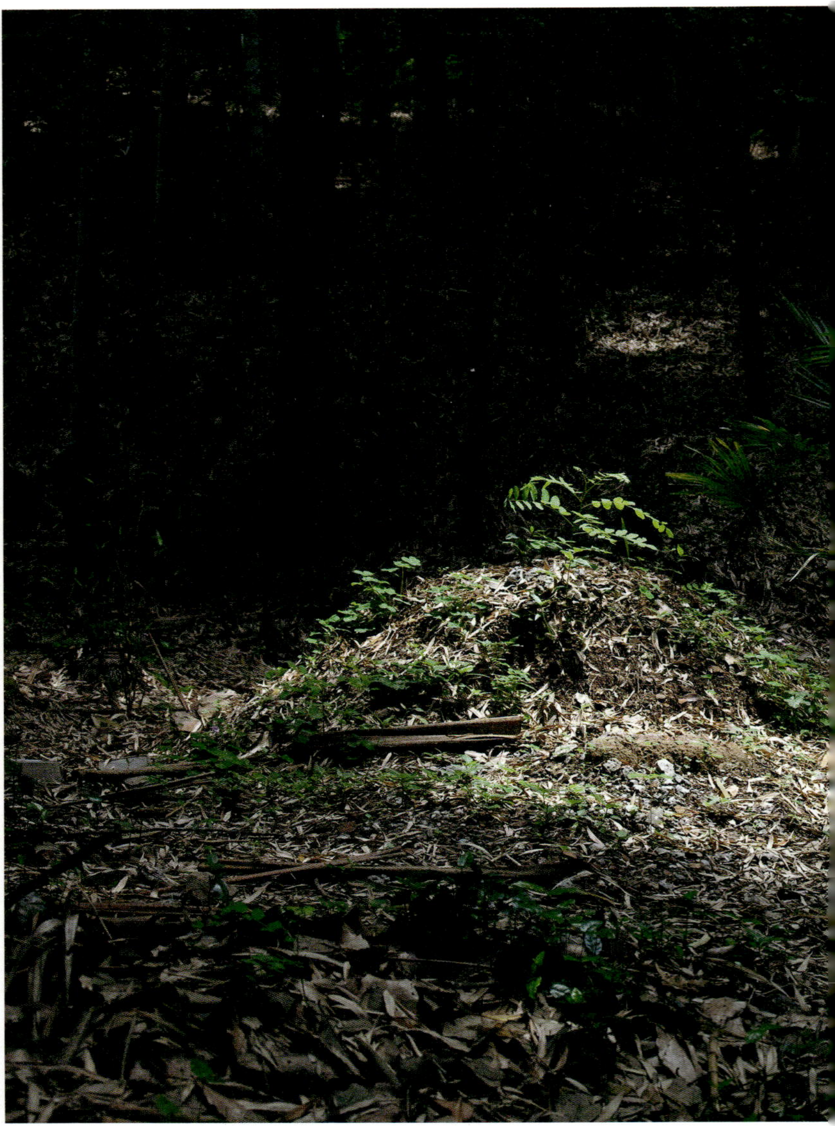

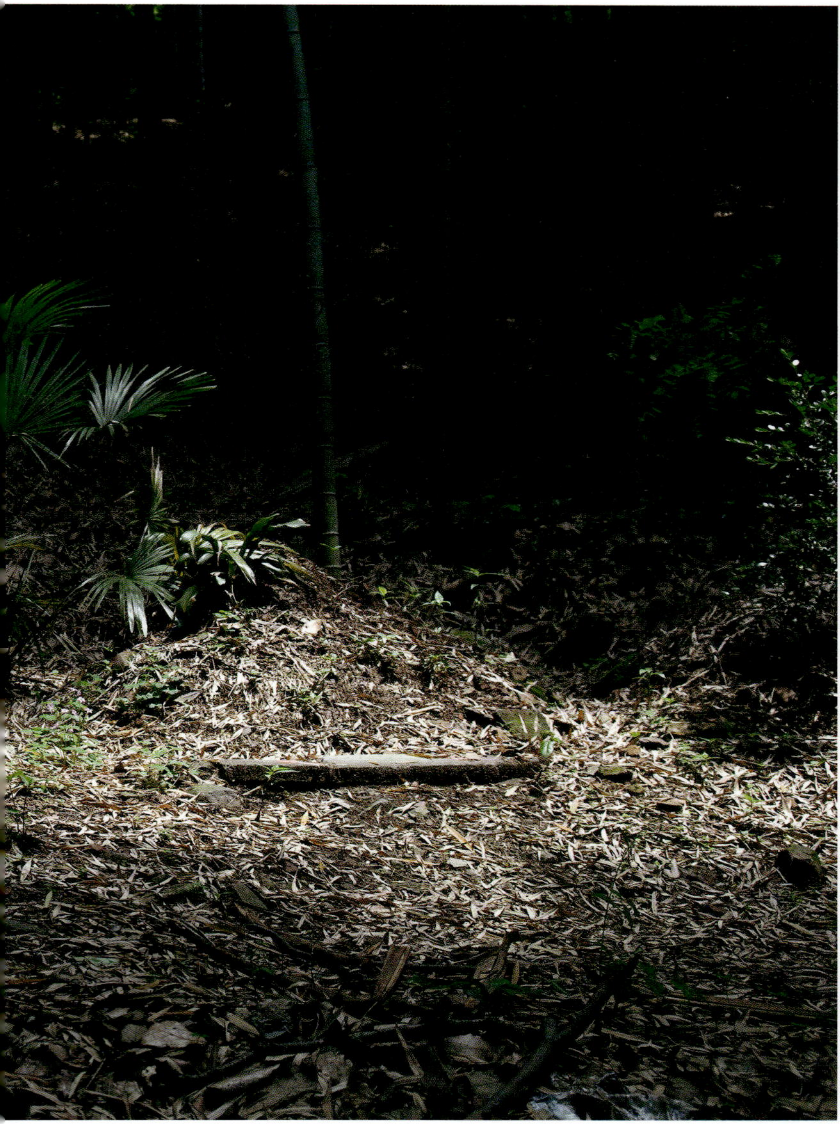

8

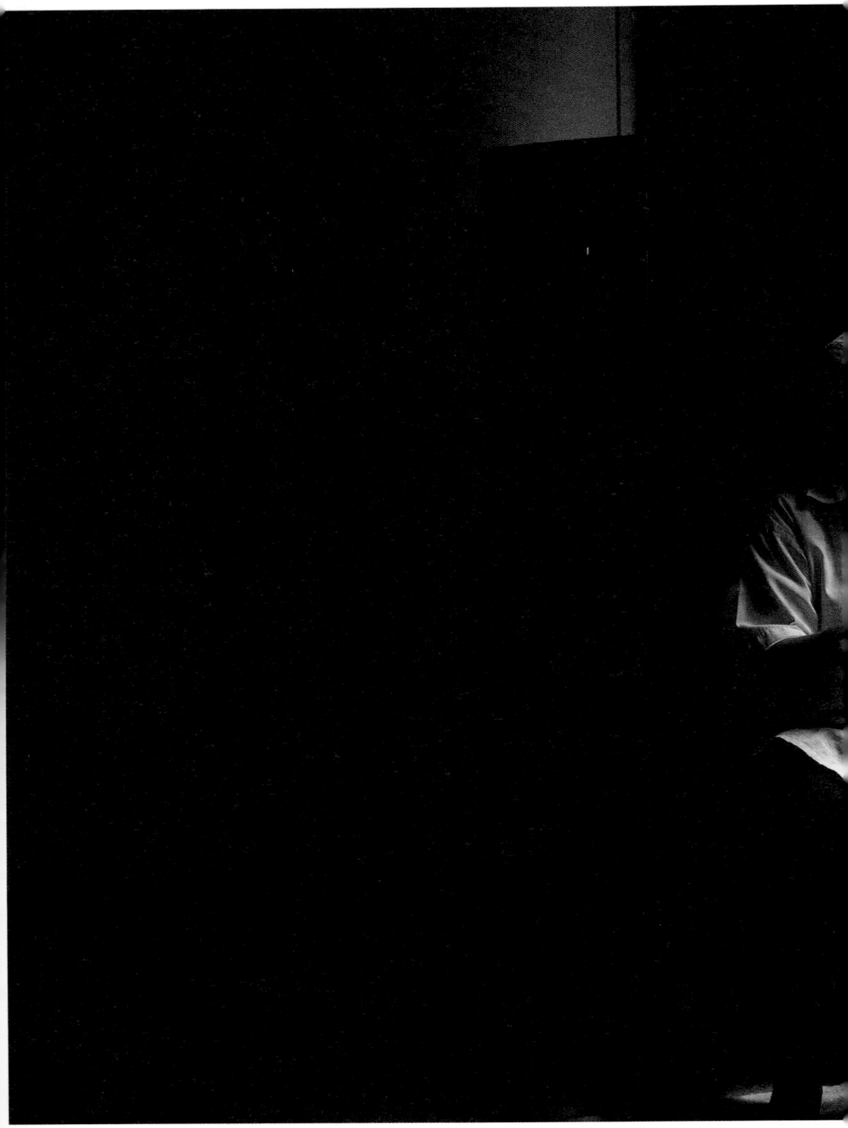

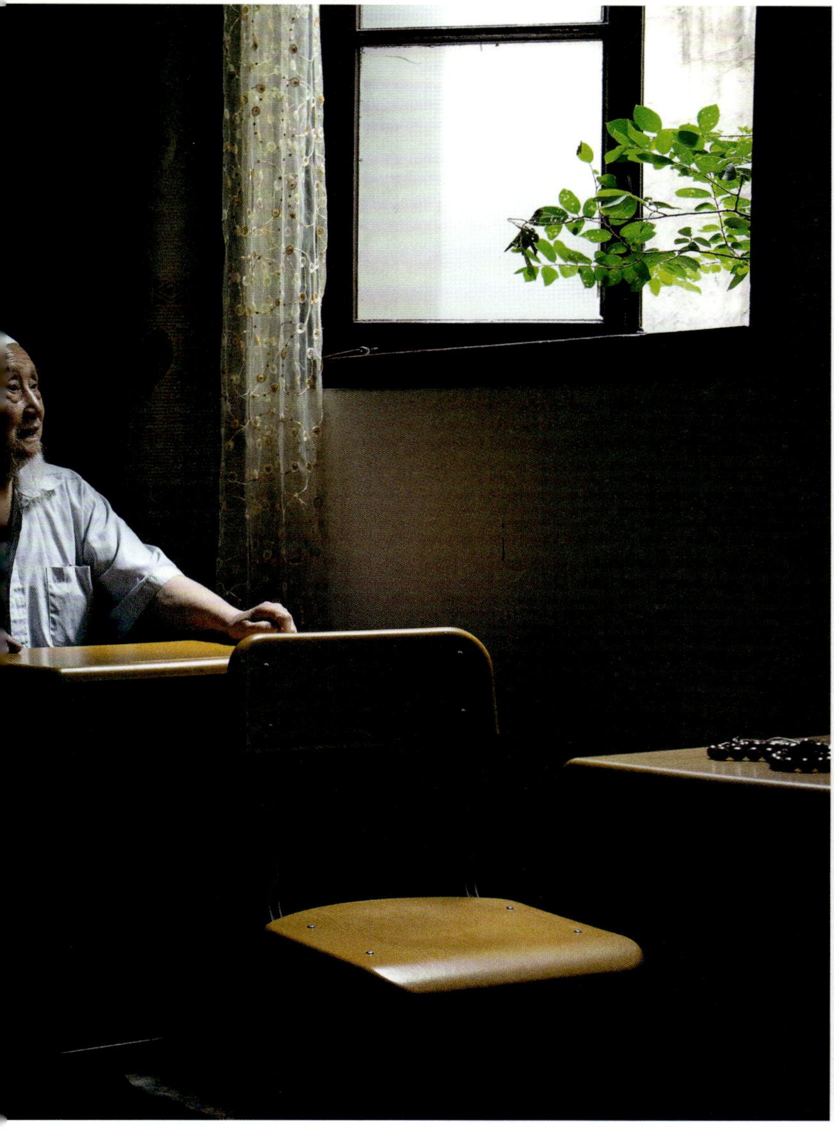

9

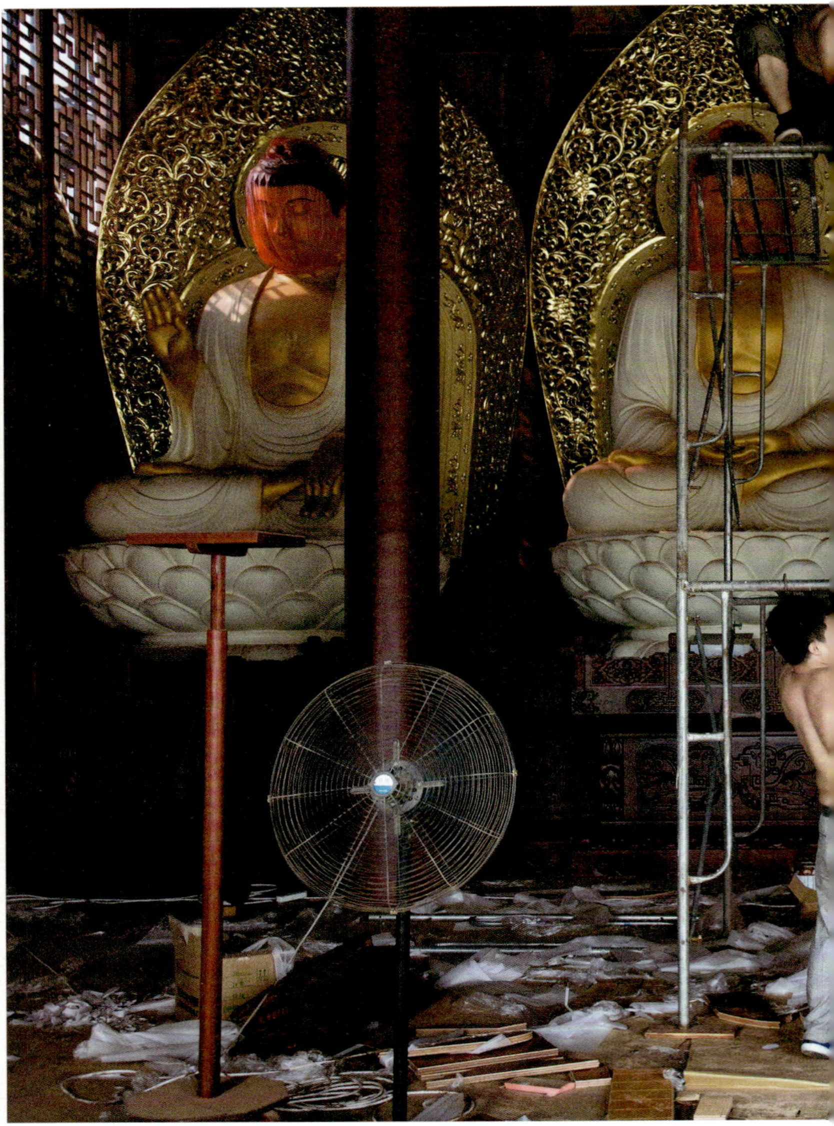

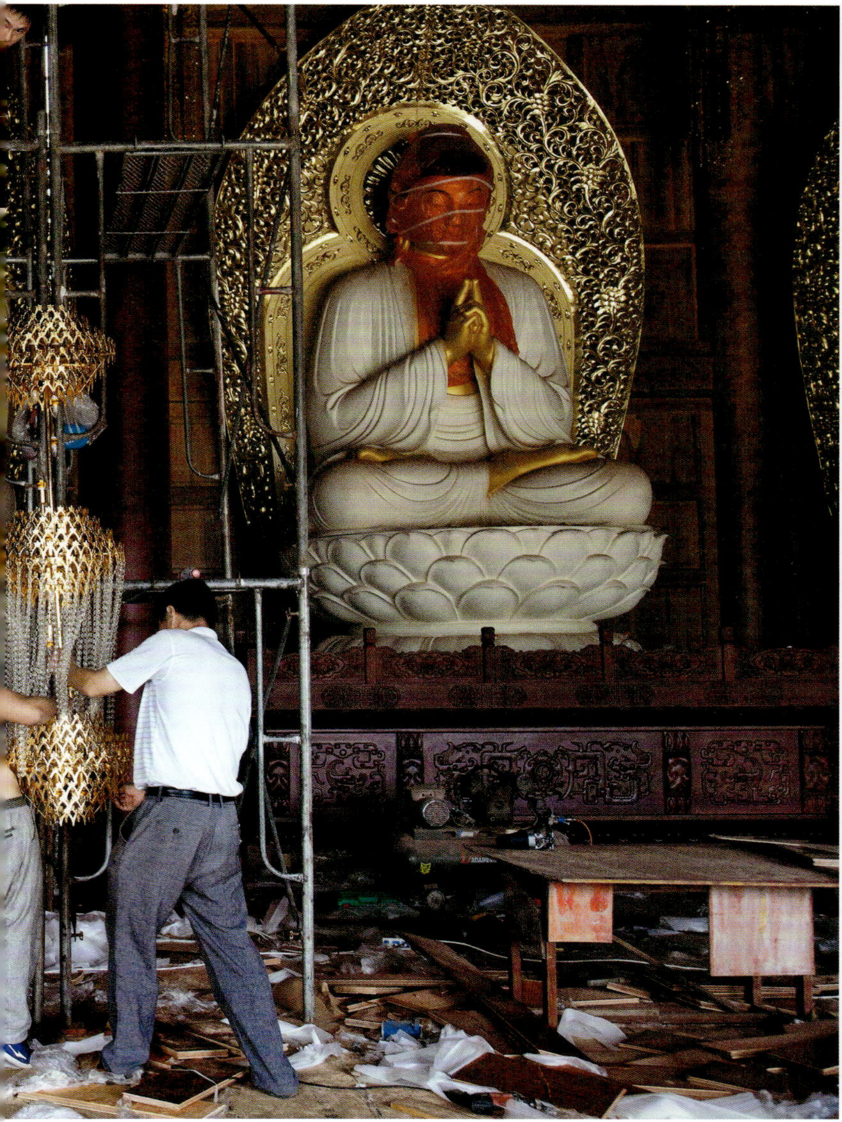

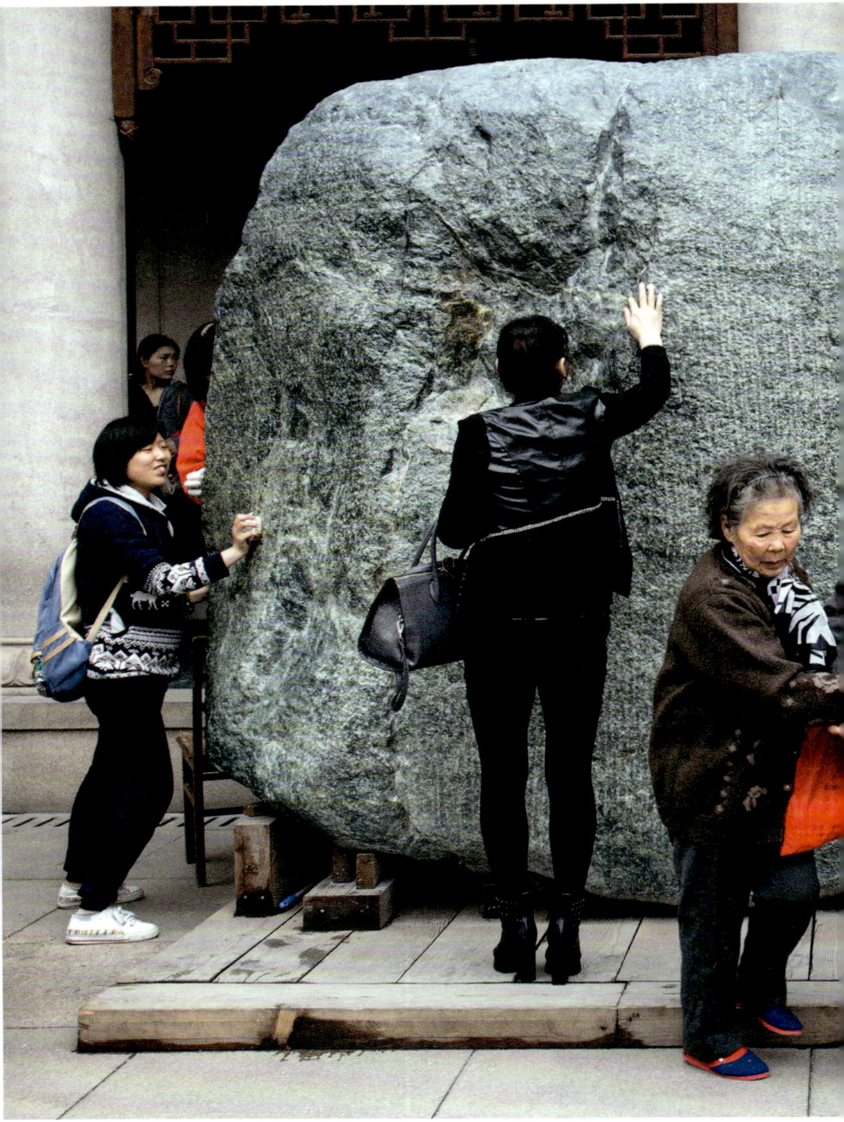

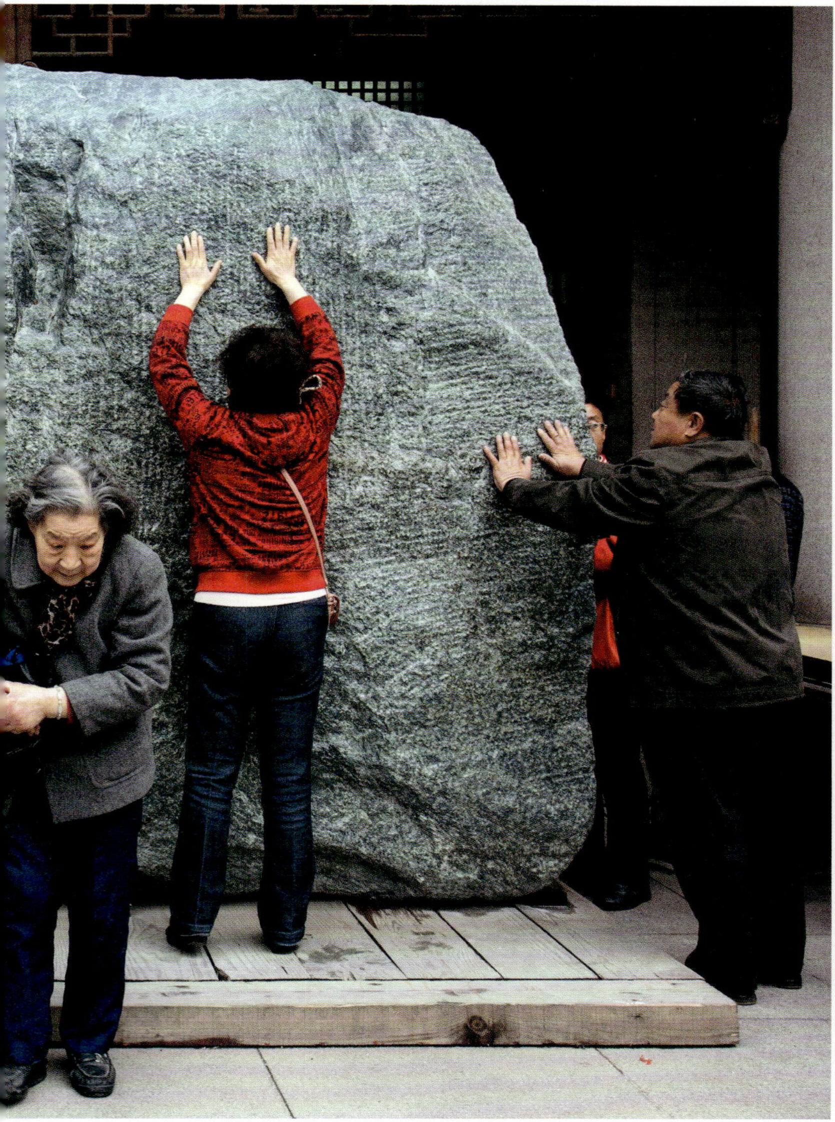

11

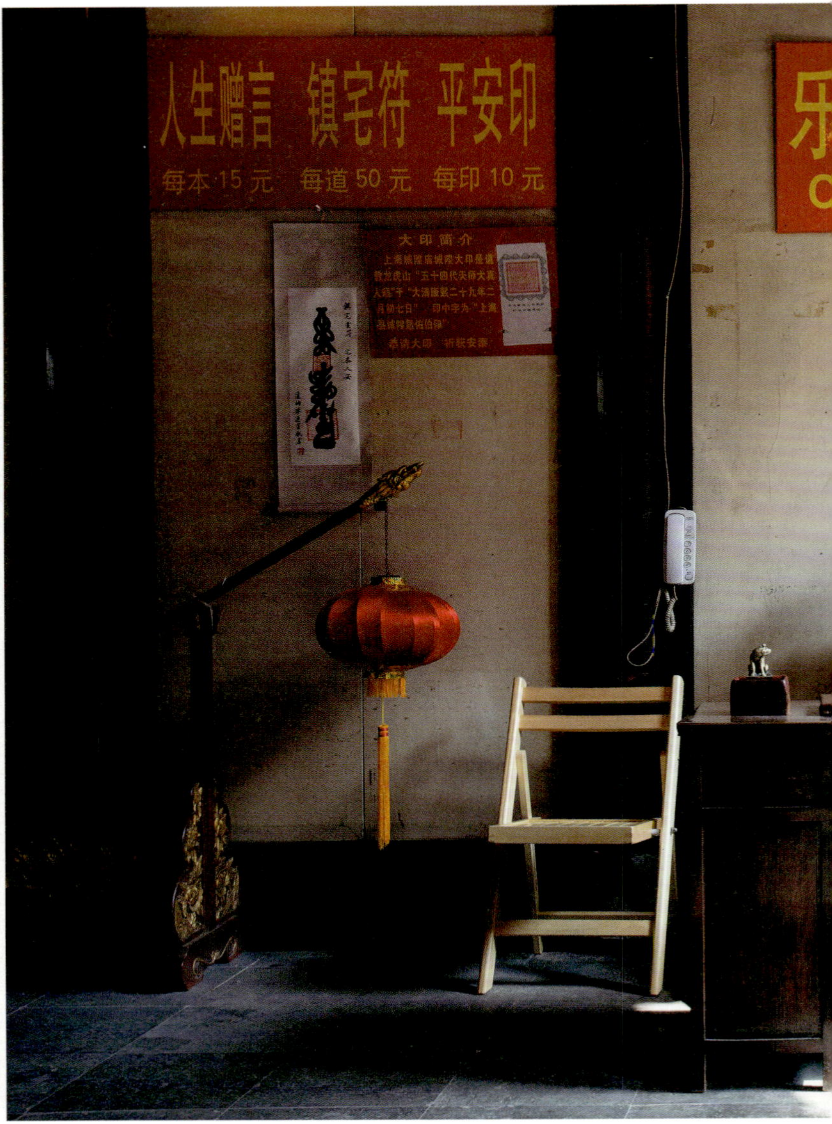
人生赠言 镇宅符 平安印
每本15元 每道50元 每印10元
大印简介

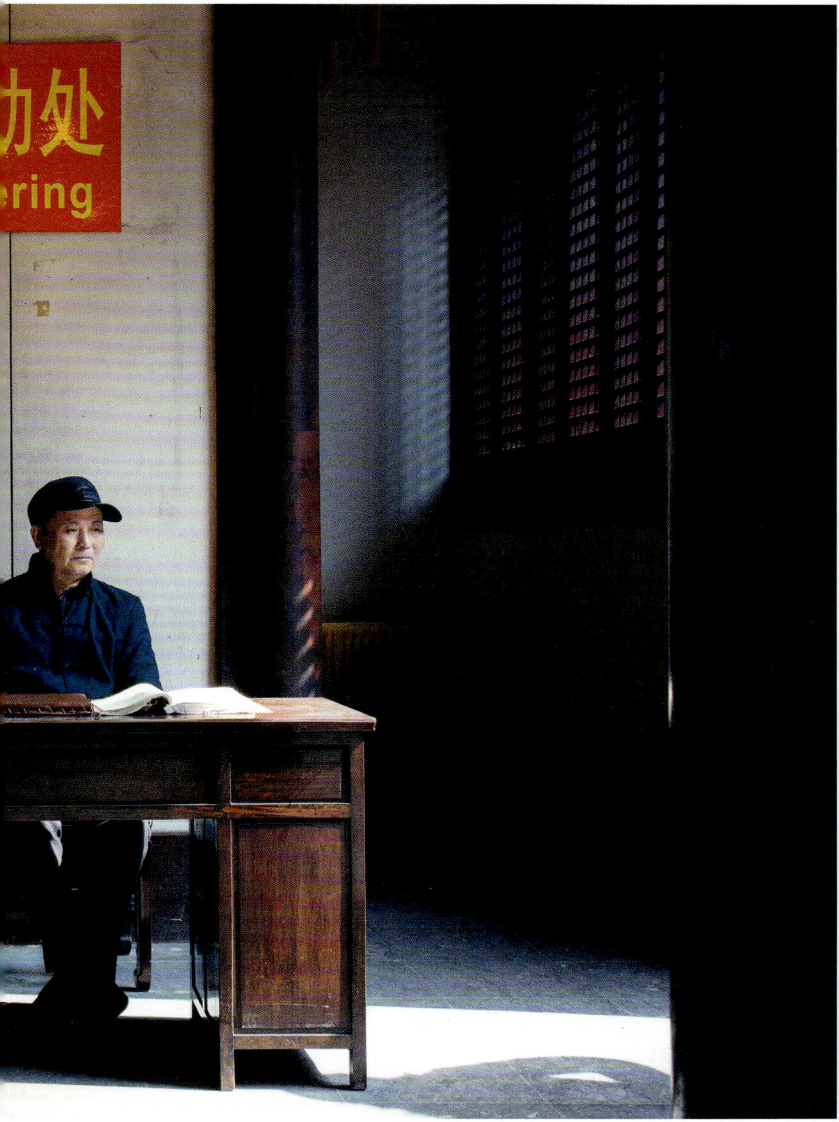
处
ering

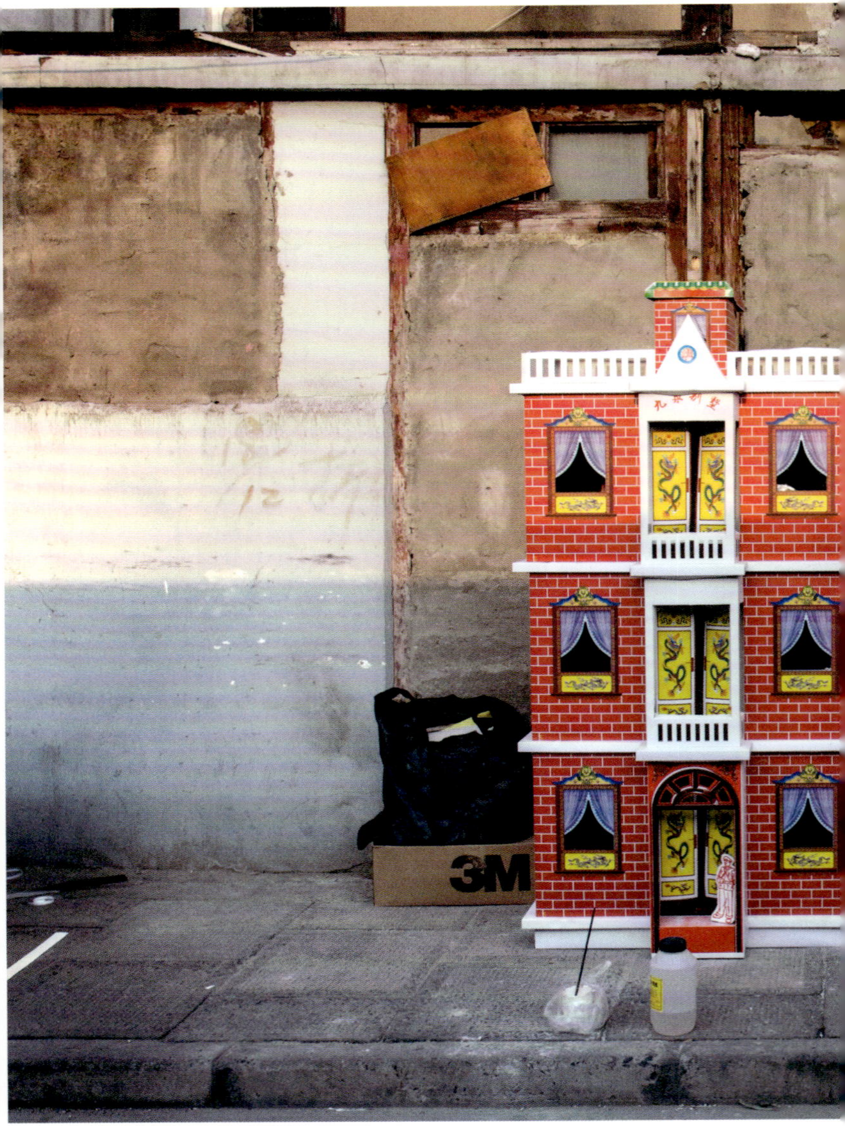
3M

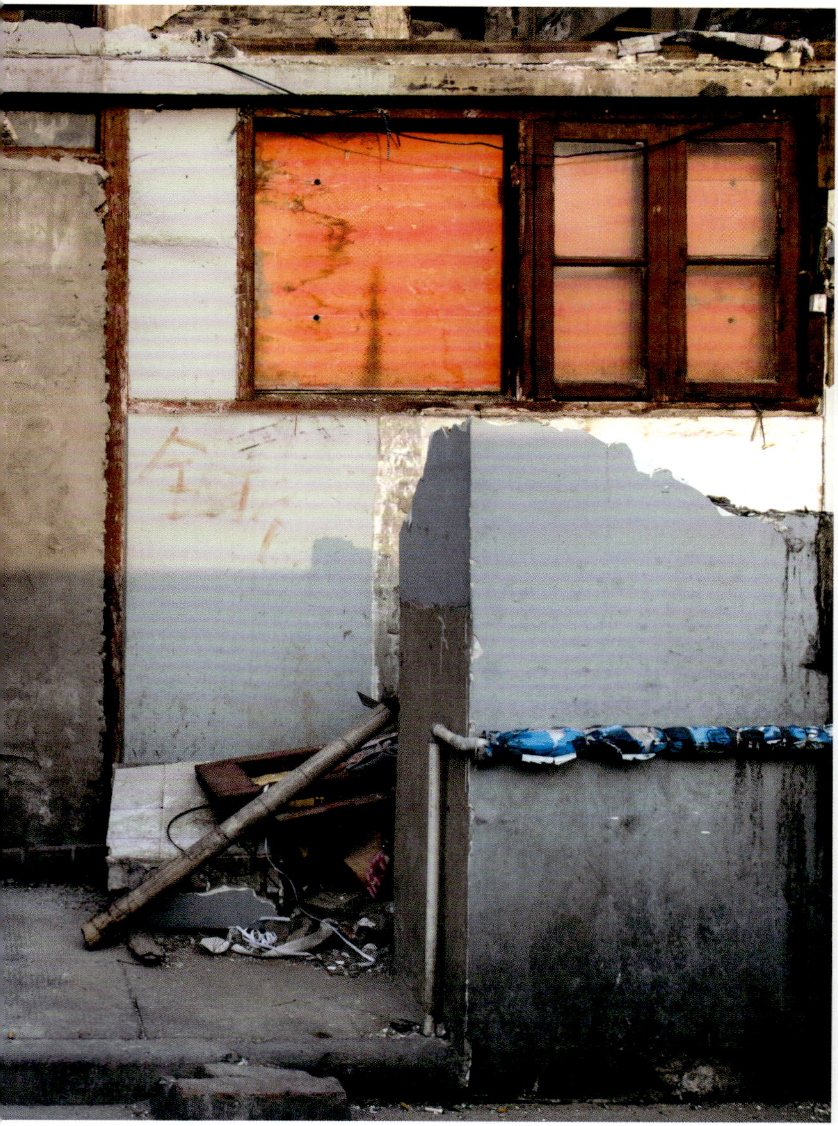

13

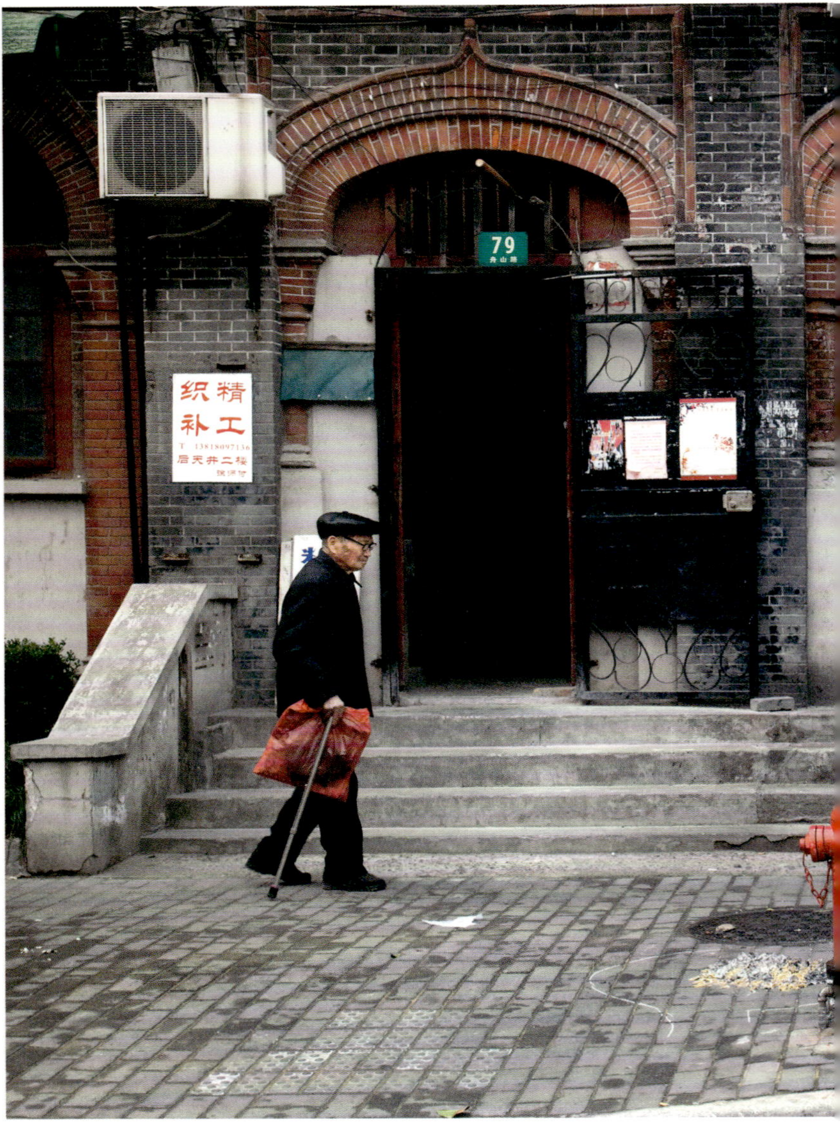
79
舟山路
精工
织补
T 13818097136
后天井二楼
张师付

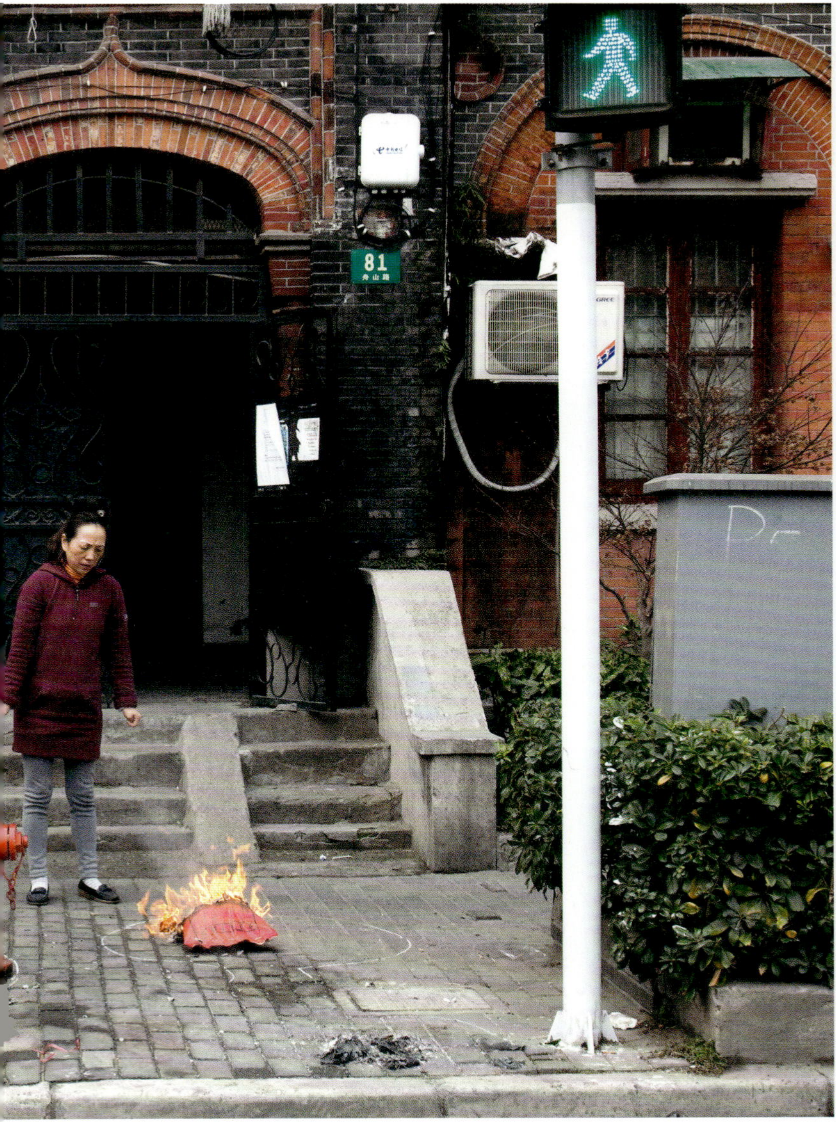
81
舟山路

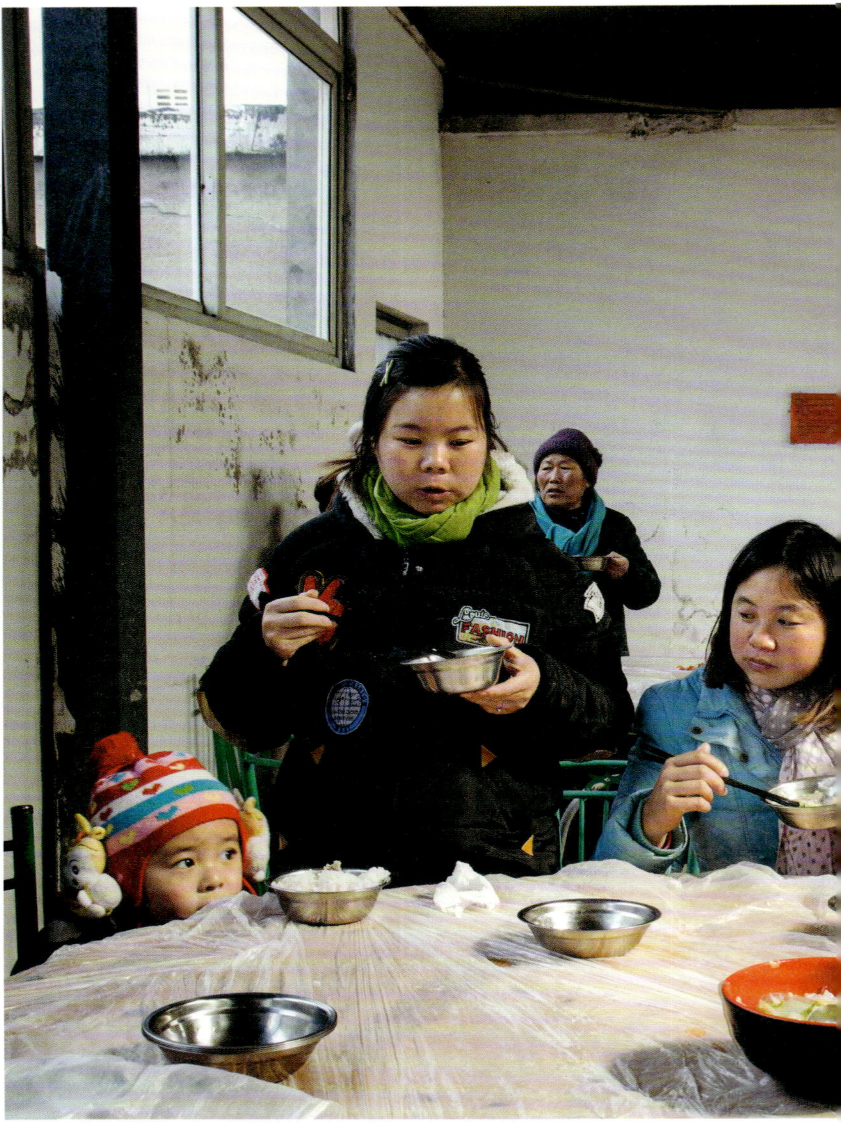
FASHION

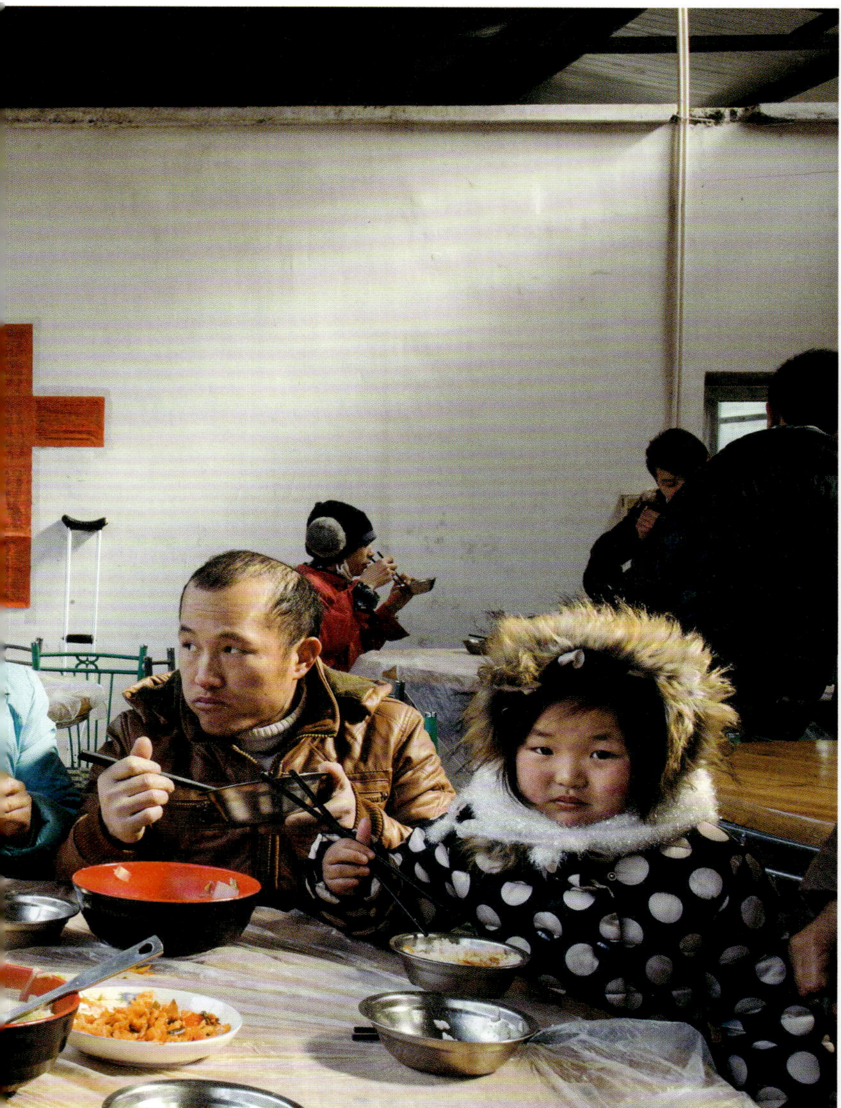

15

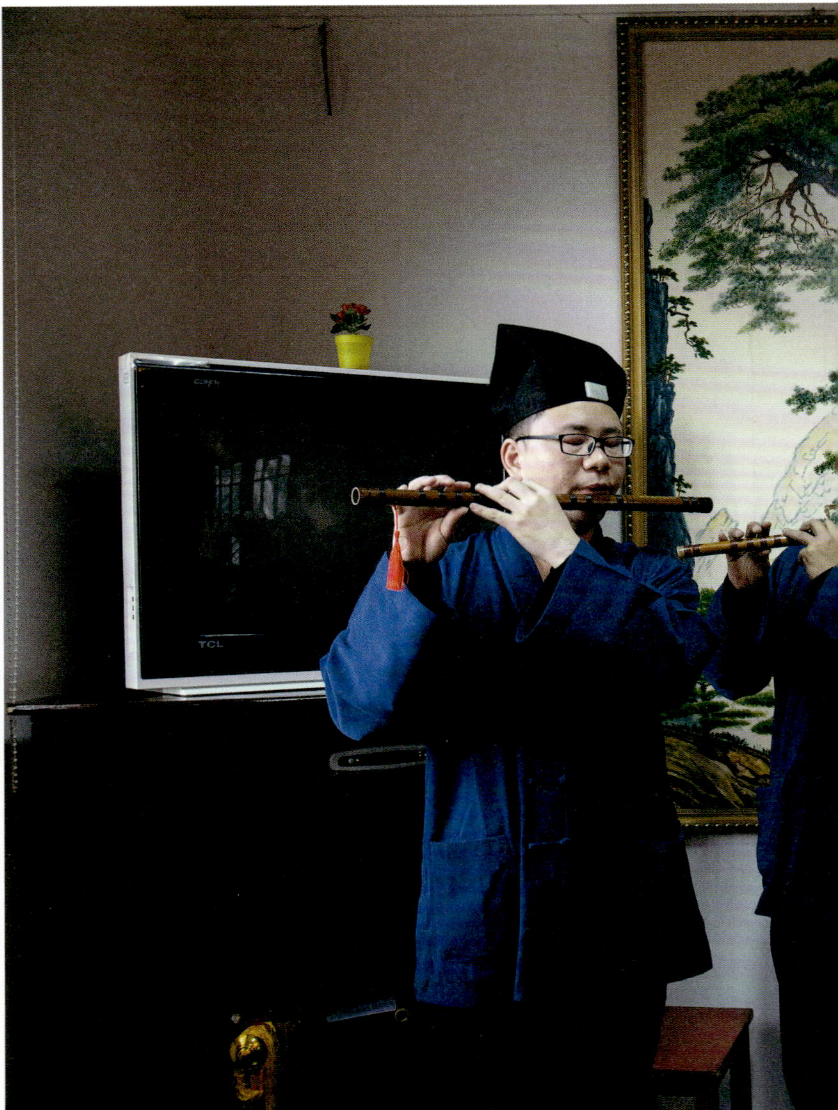
TCL

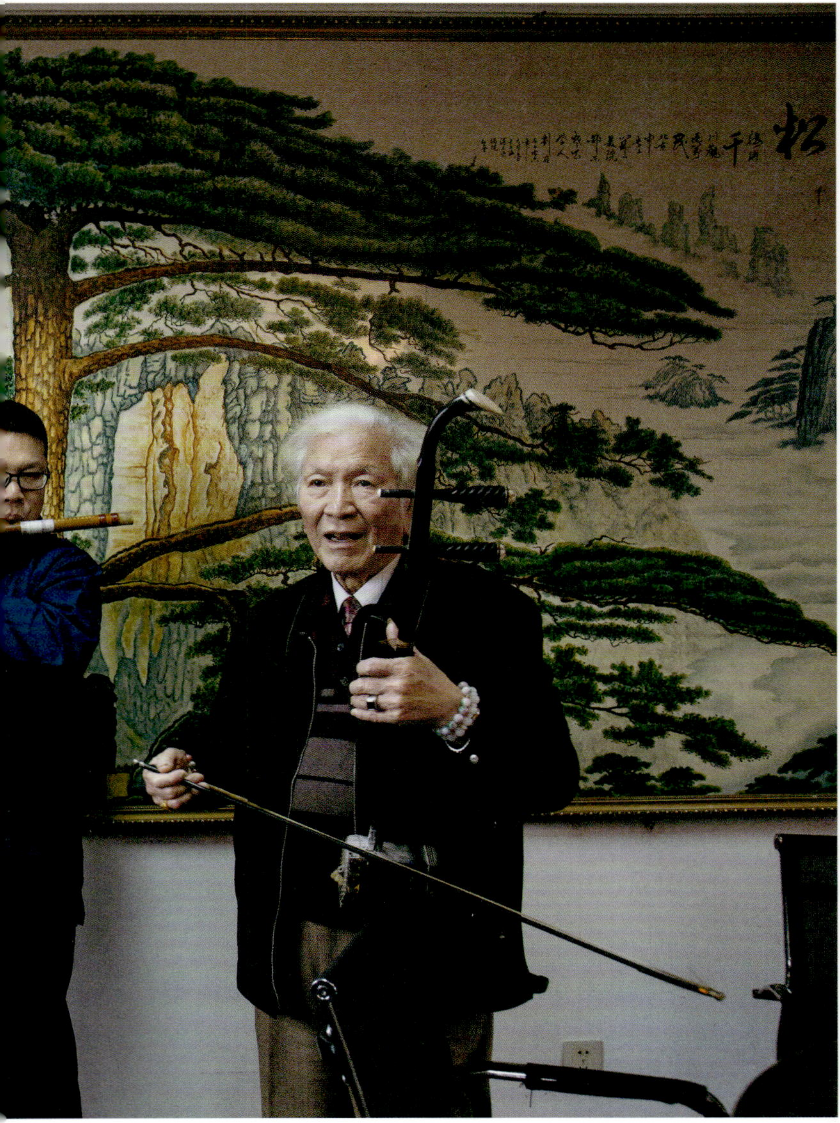

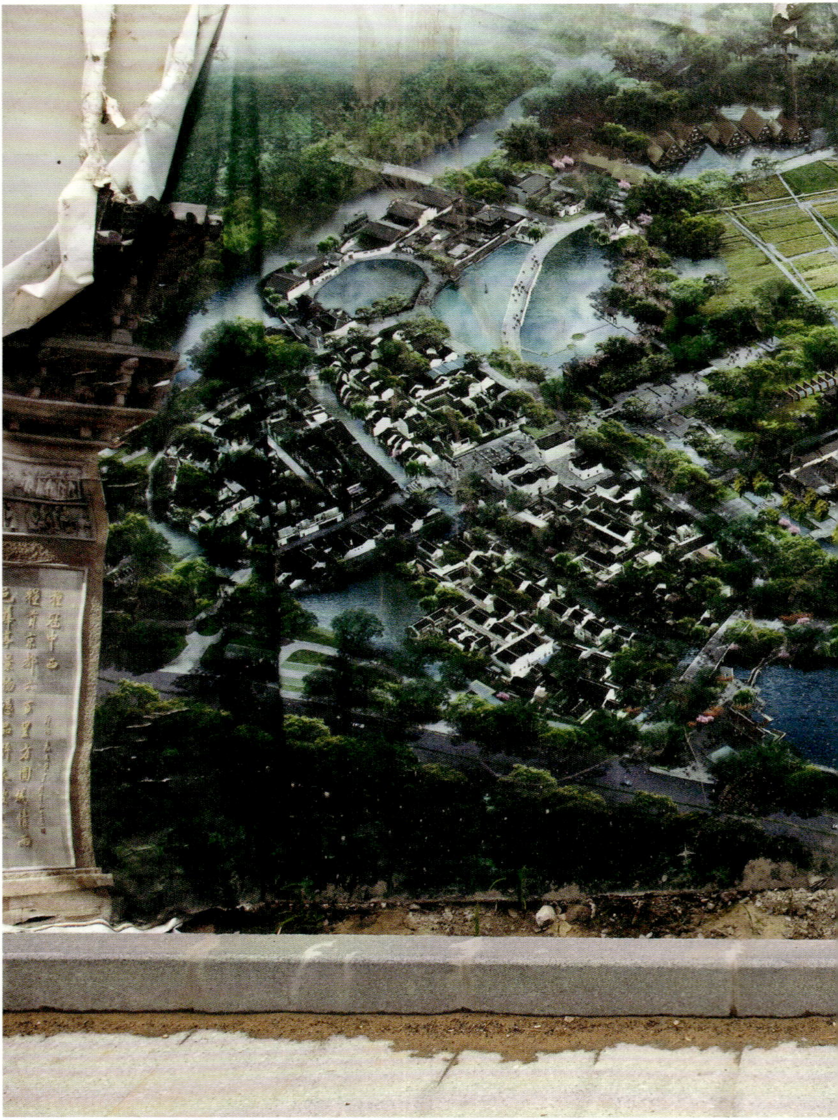

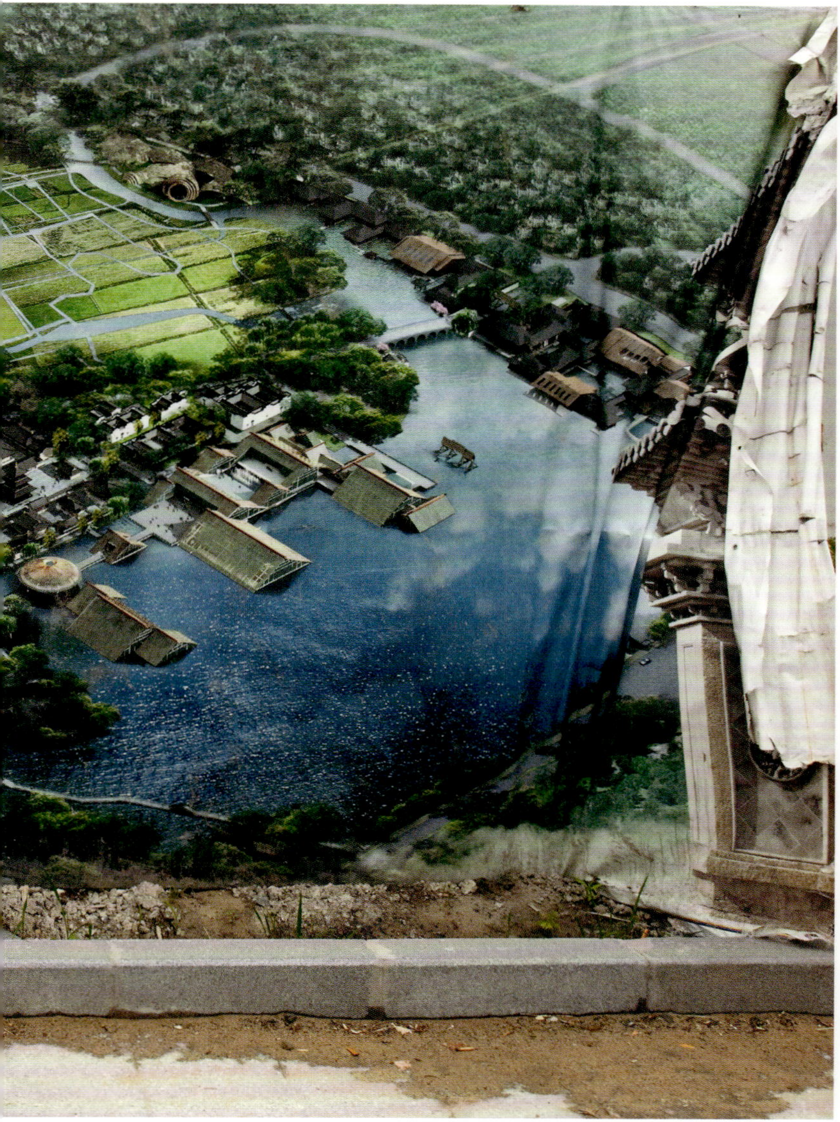

17

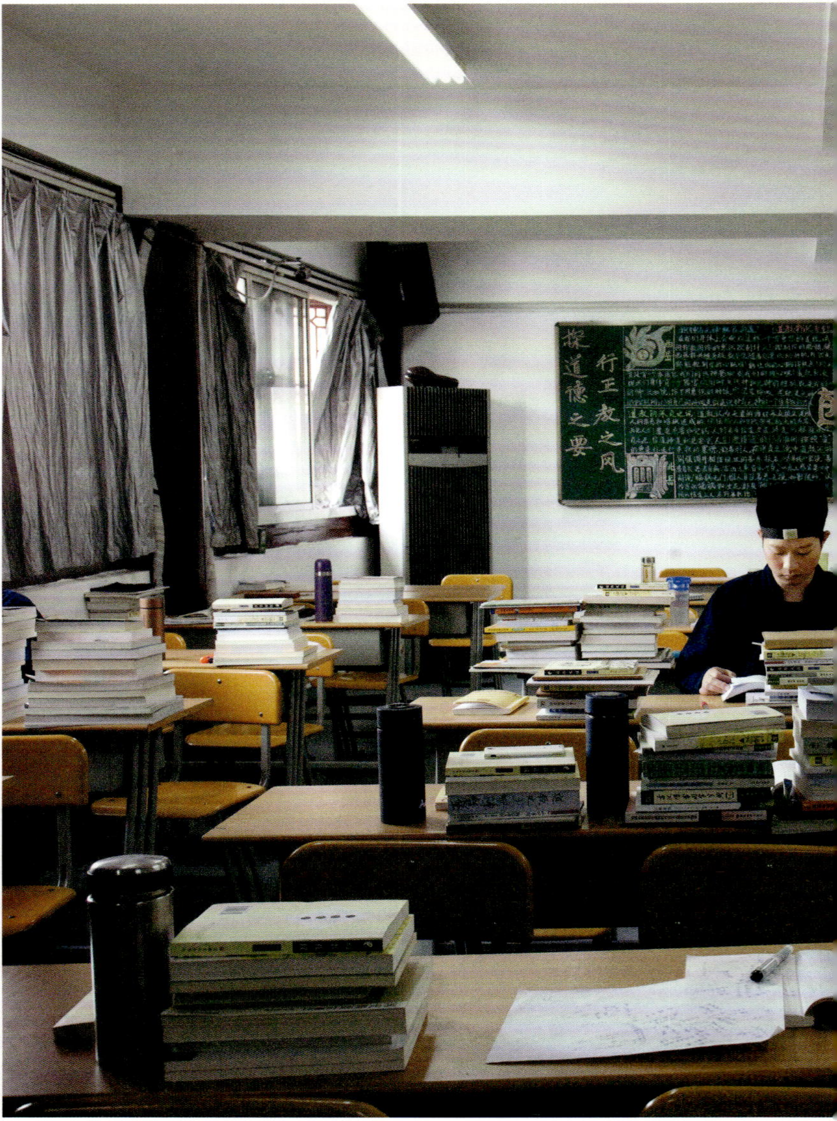
探道德之要
行正教之风

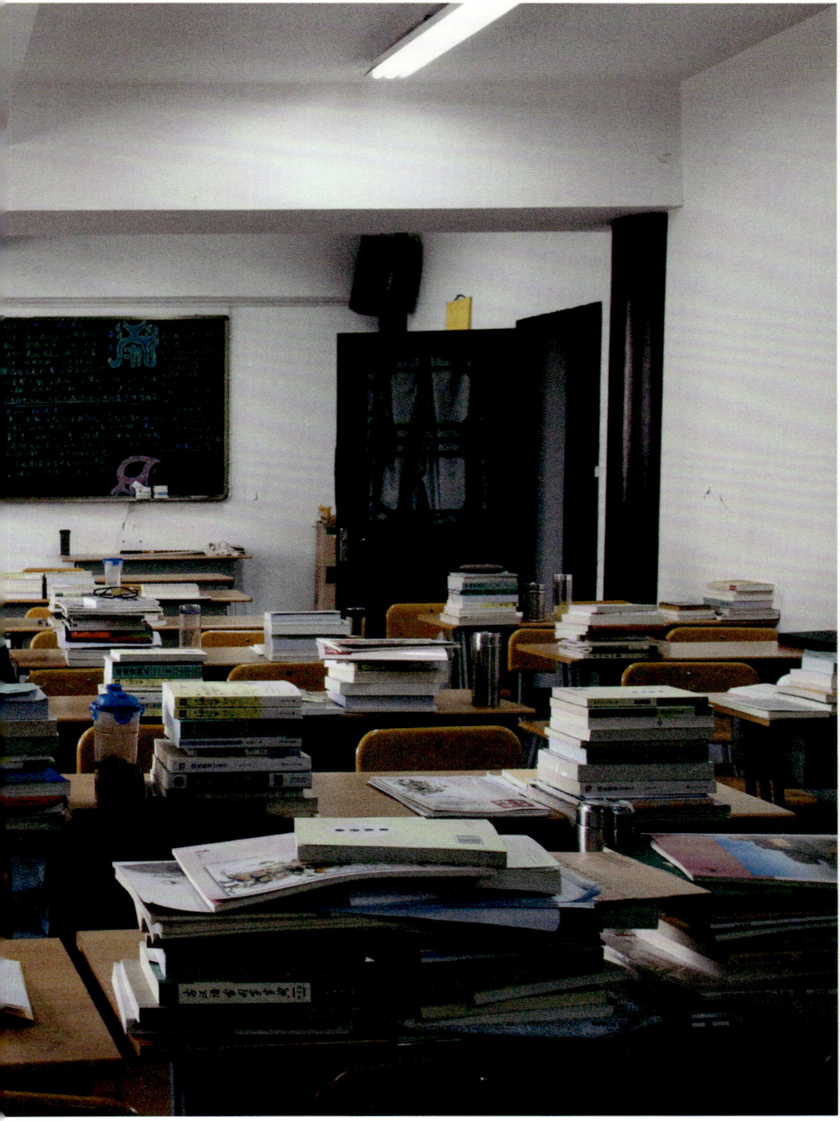

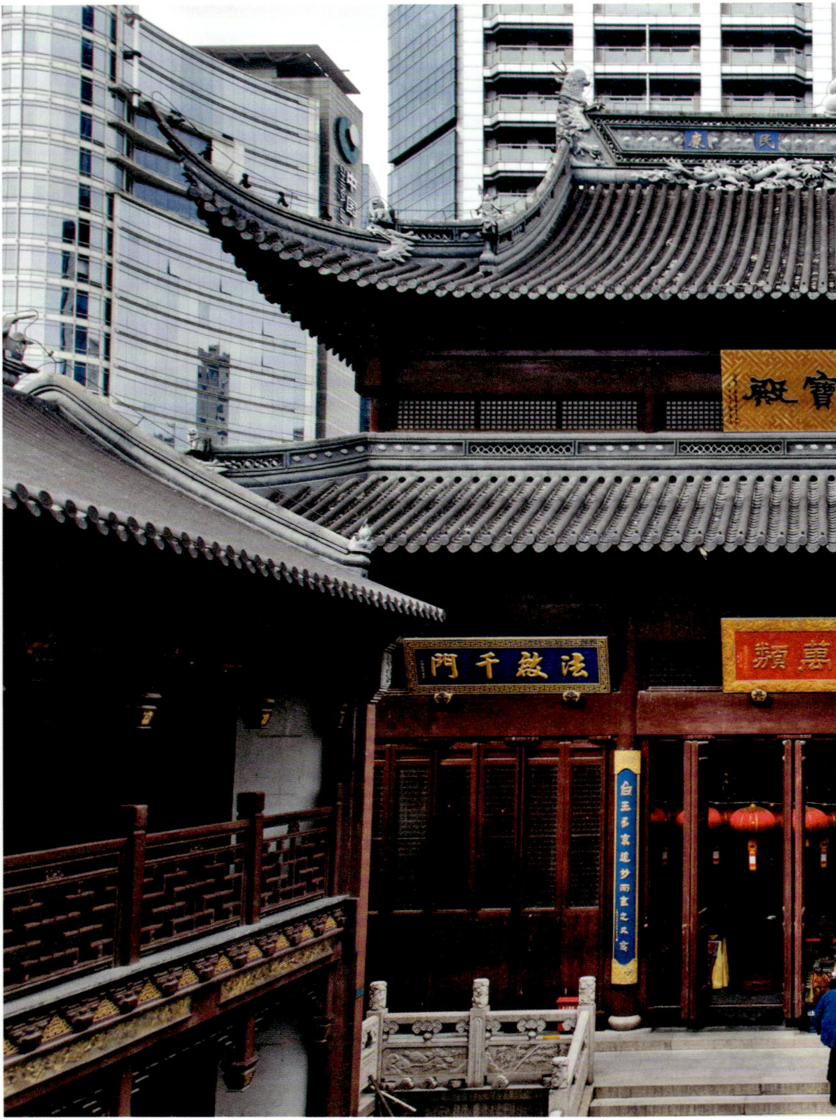

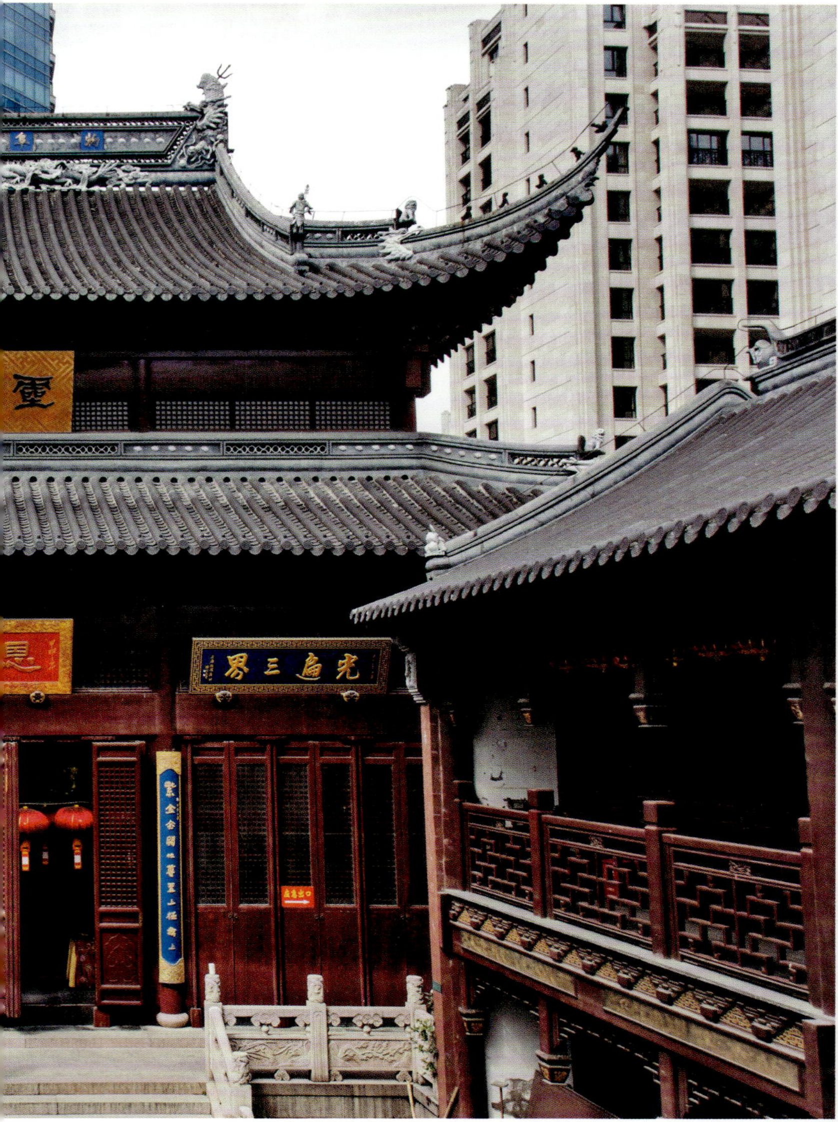
光遍三界

19

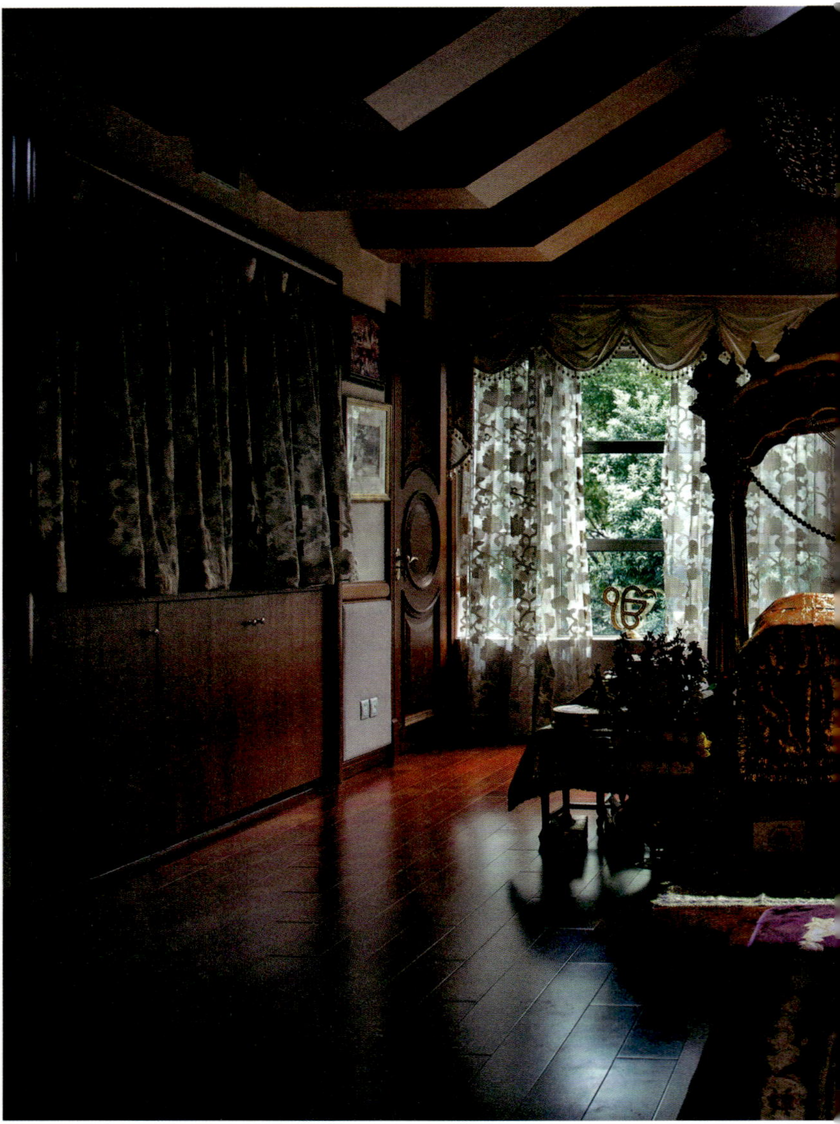

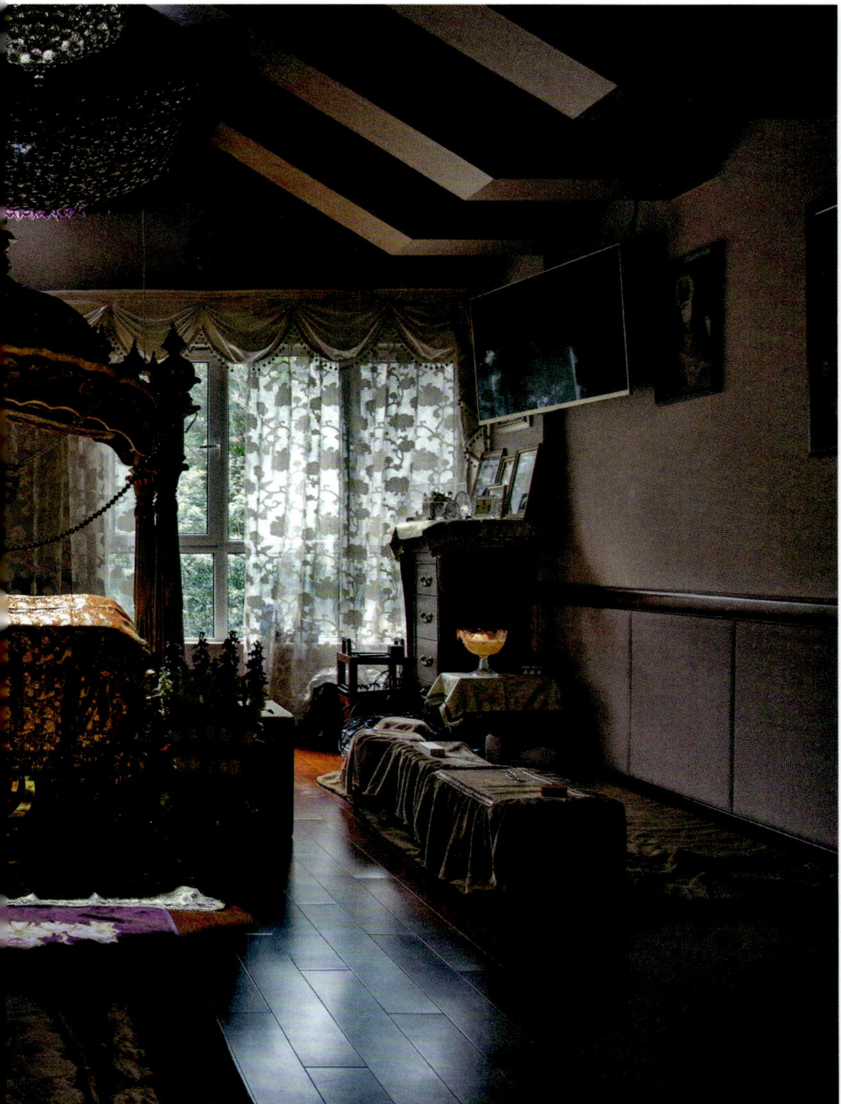

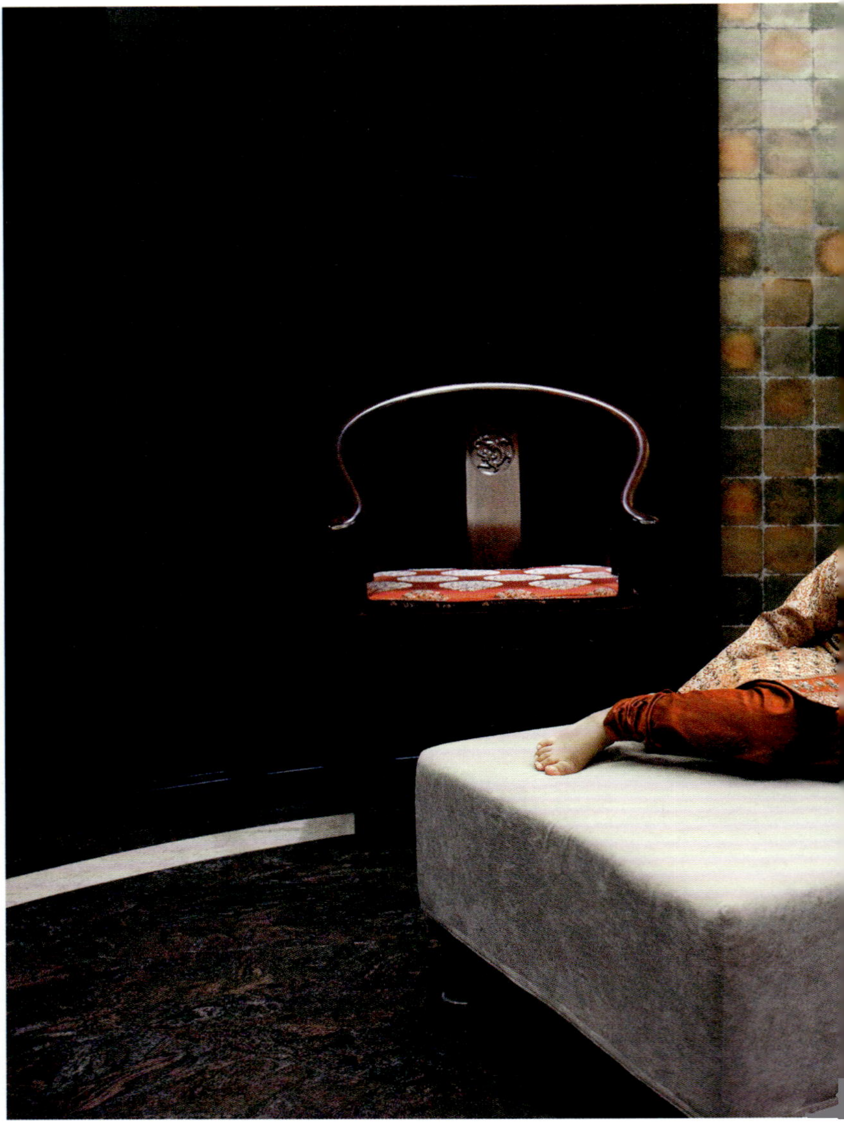

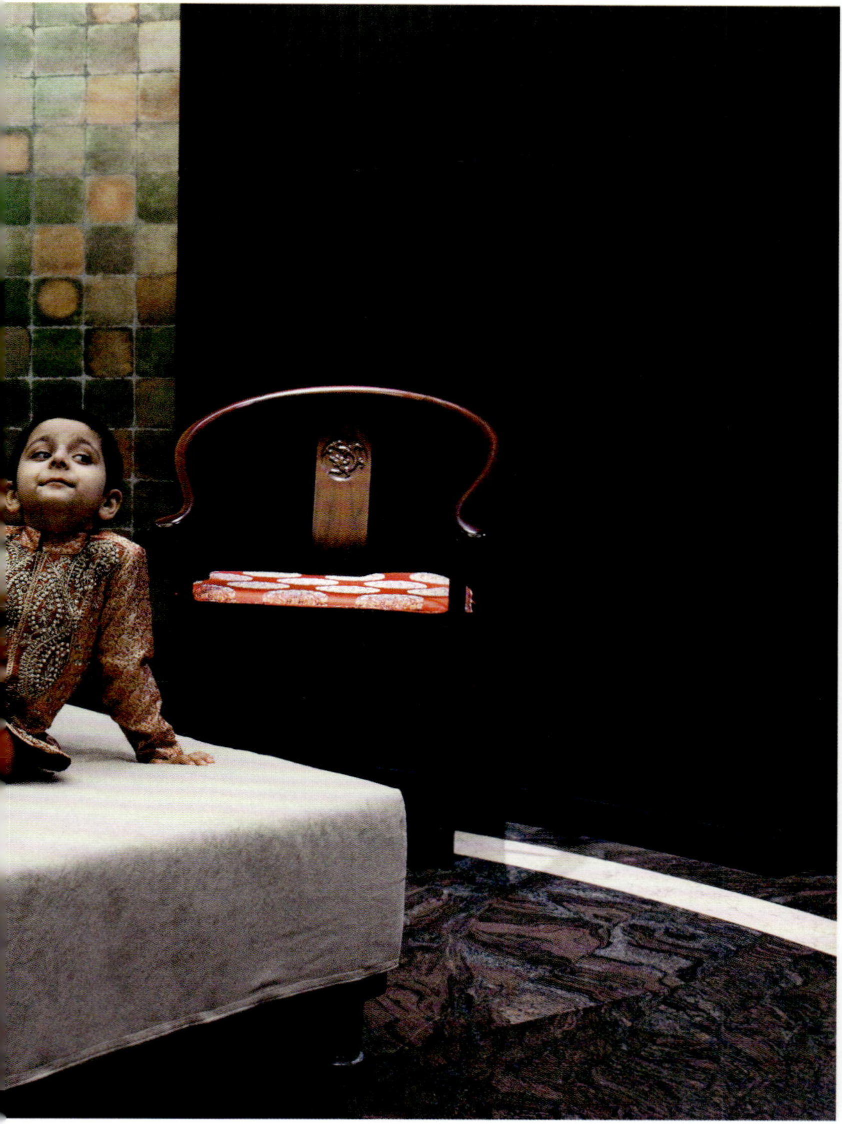

21

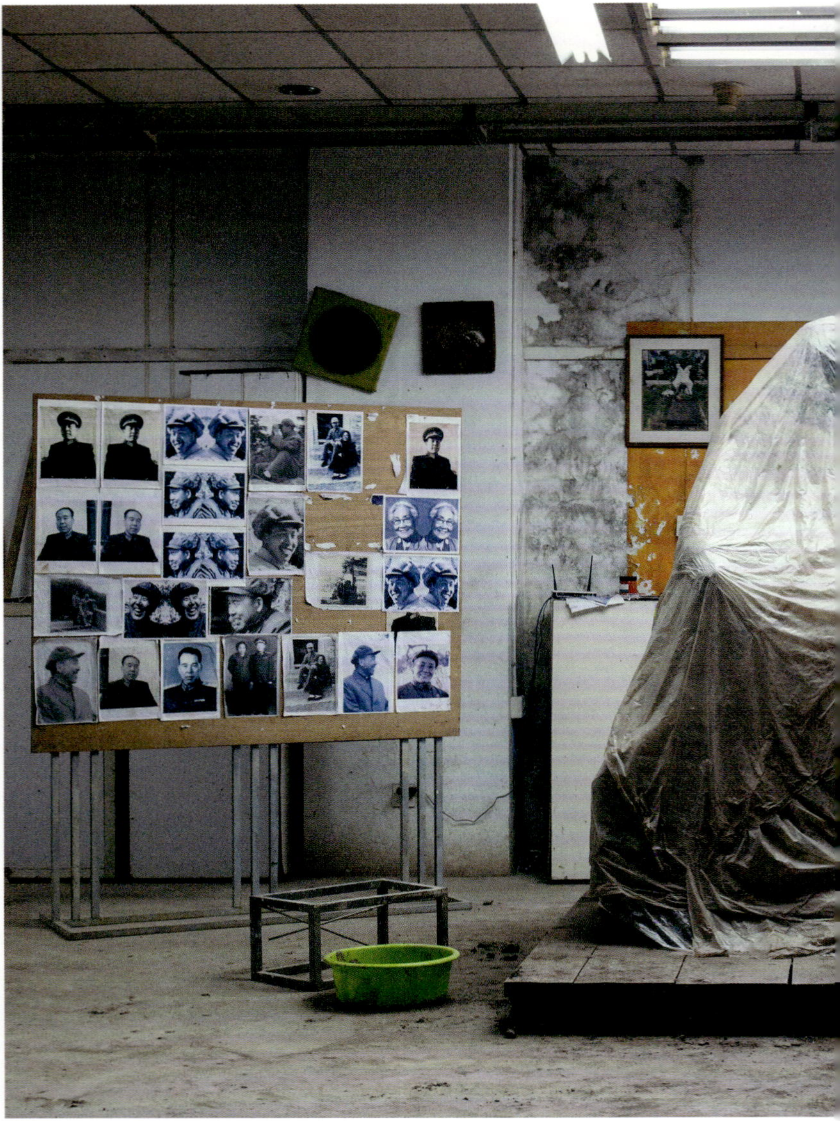

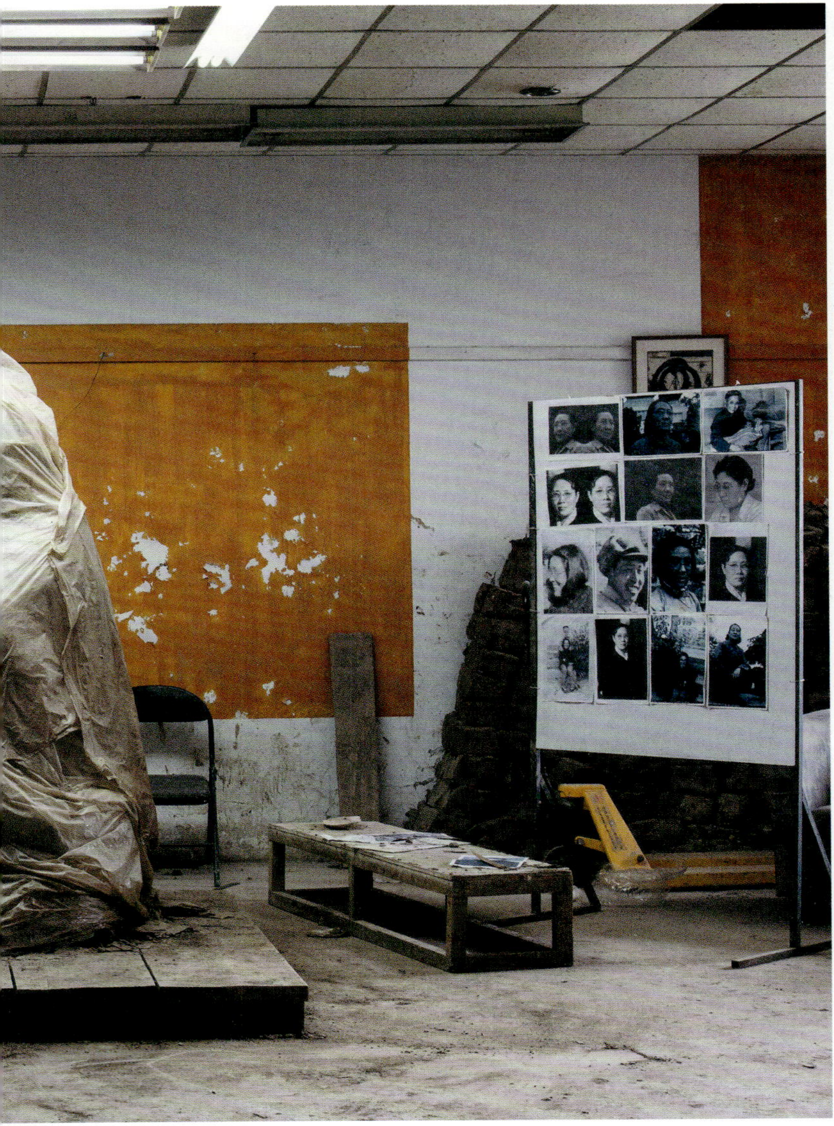

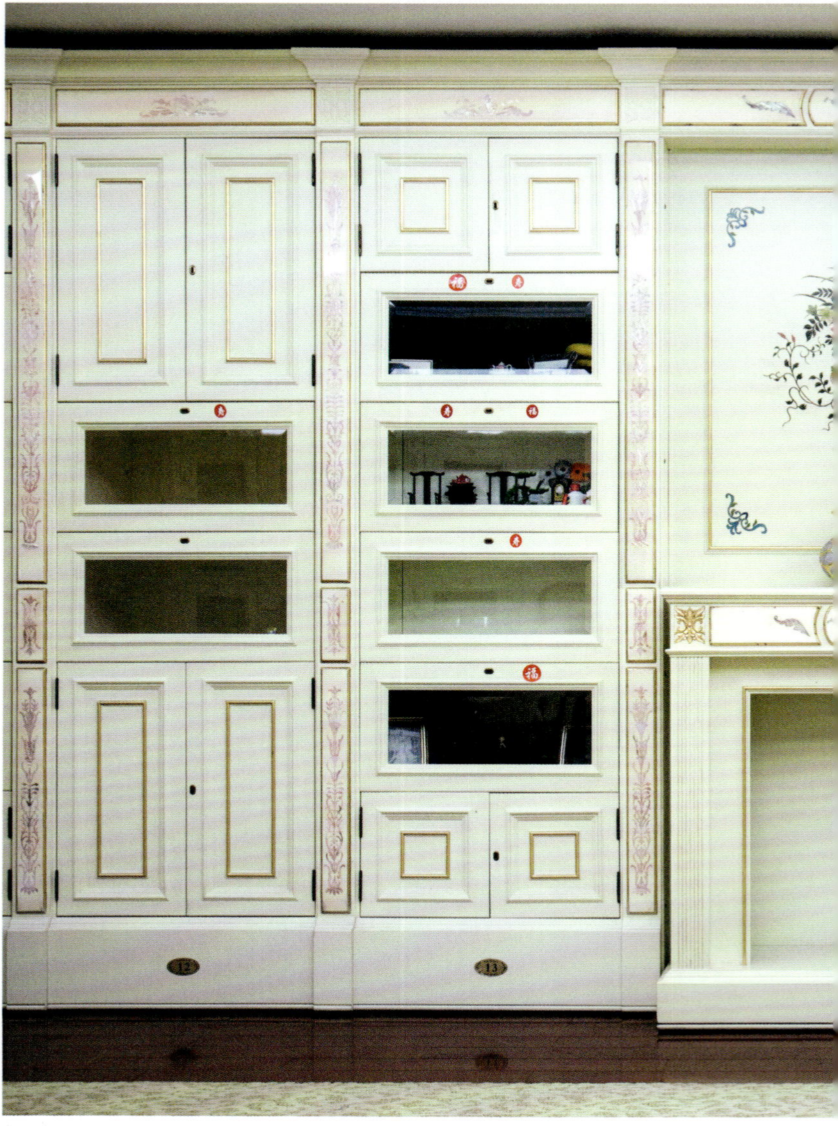

12
13

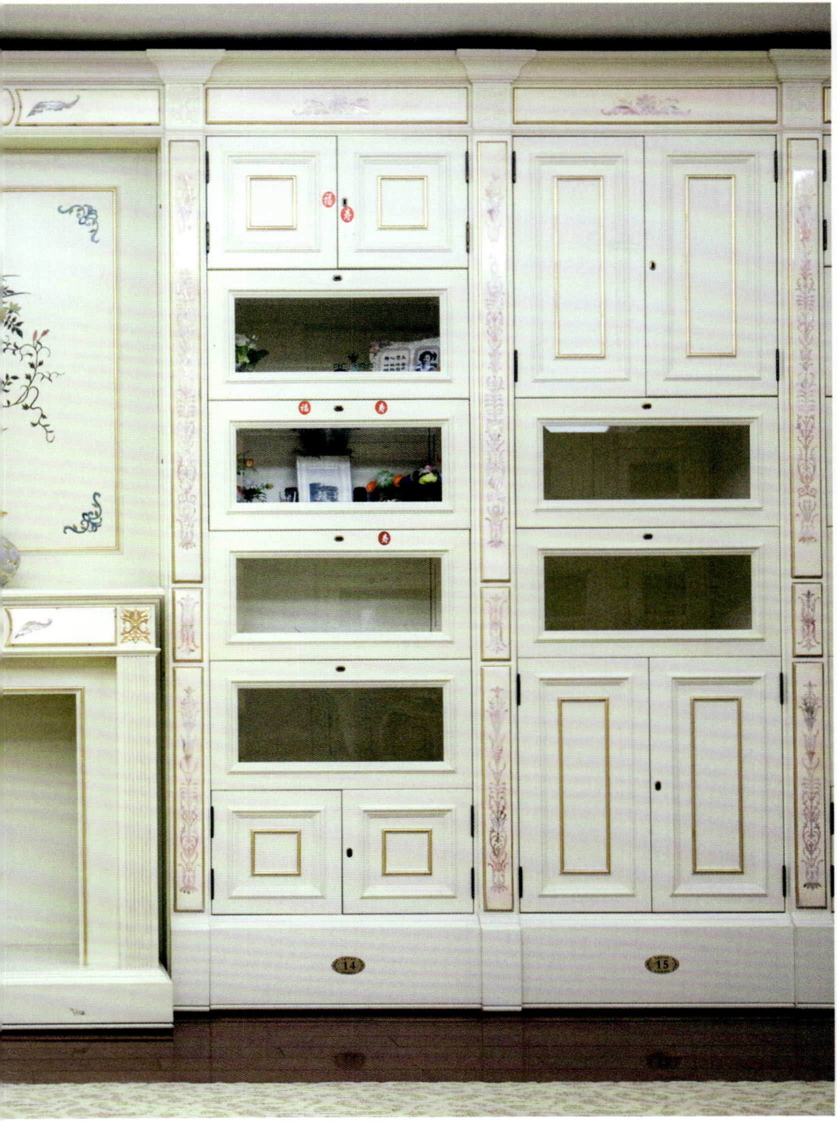
14
15

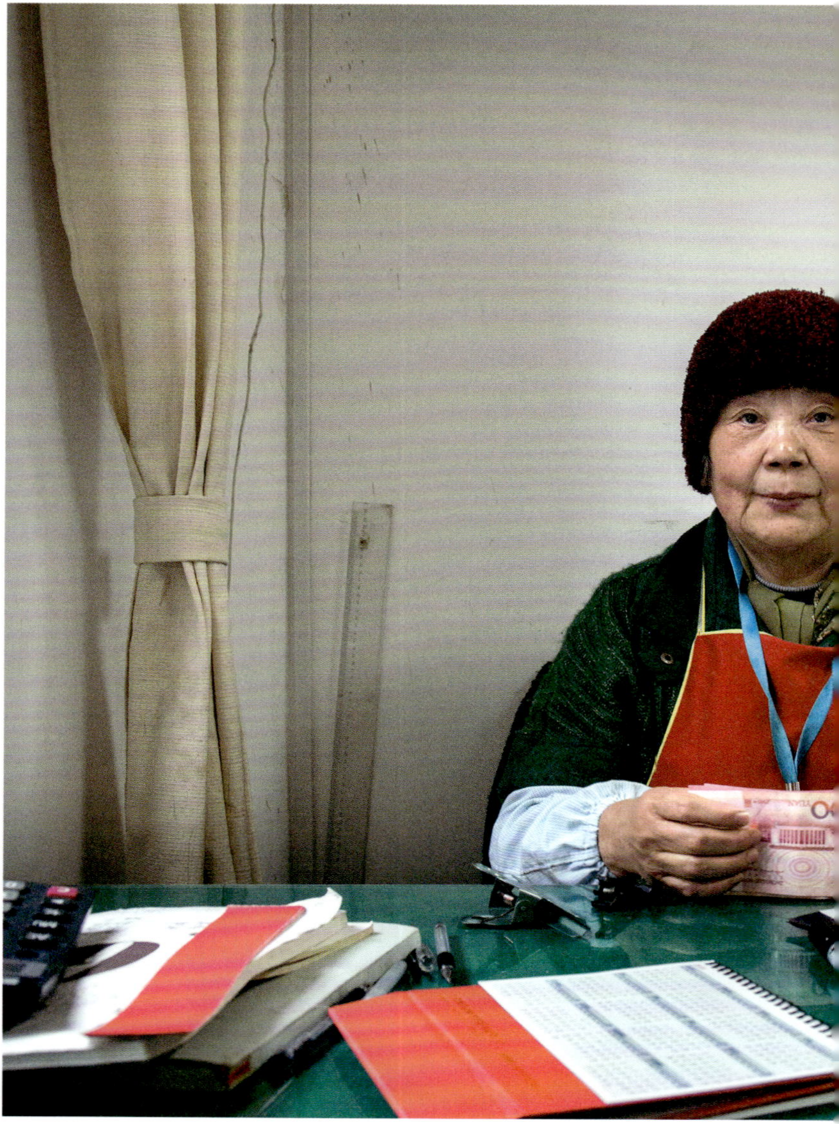

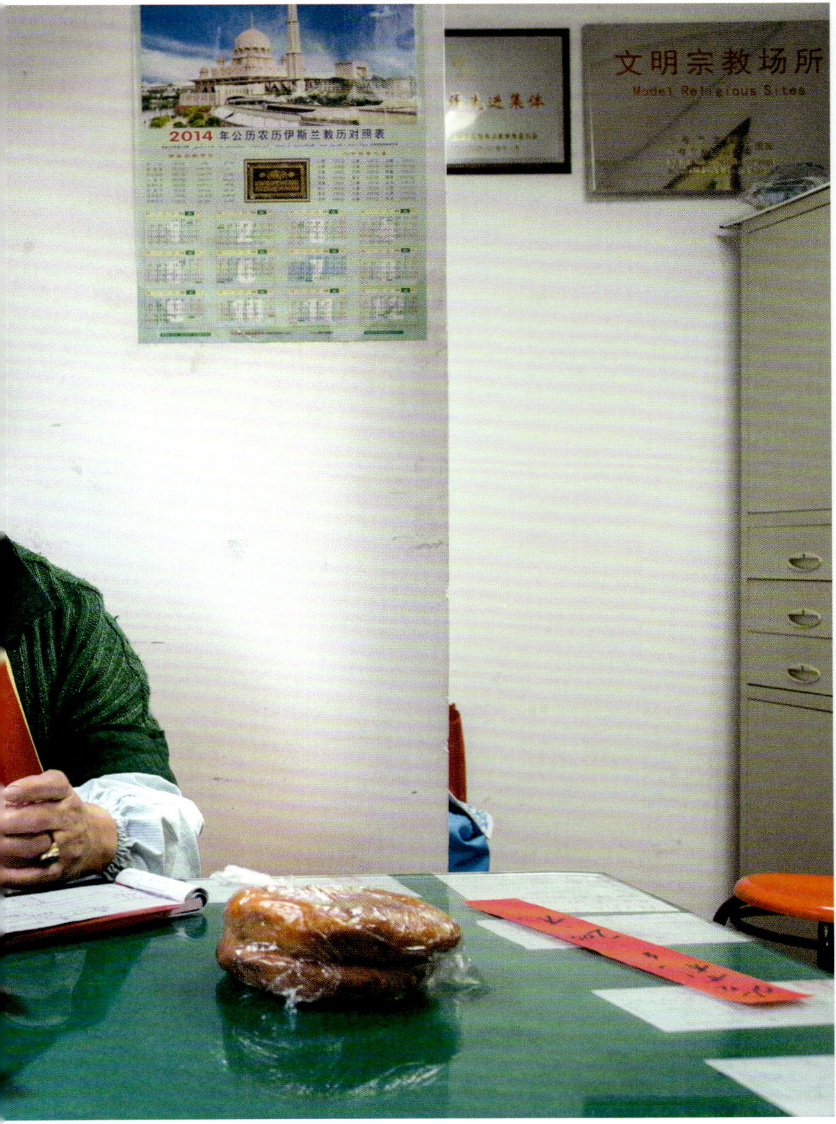
2014 年公历农历伊斯兰教历对照表
文明宗教场所
Model Religious Sites

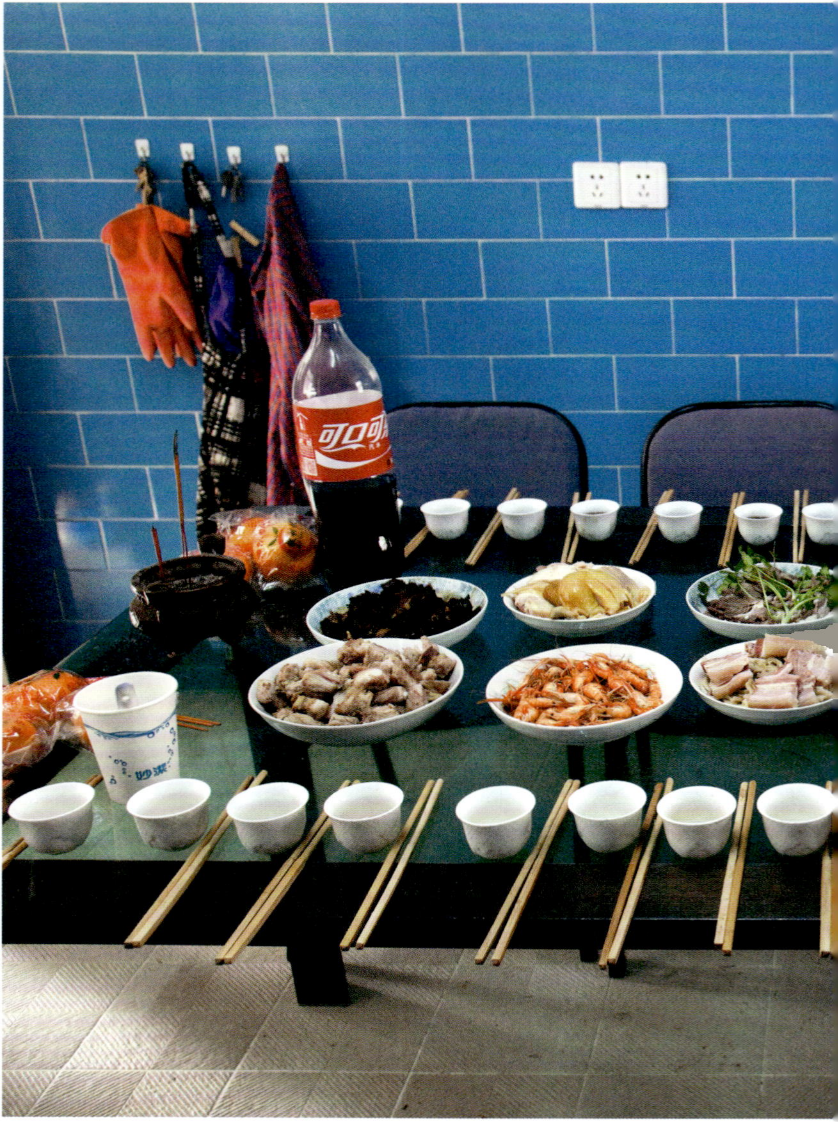

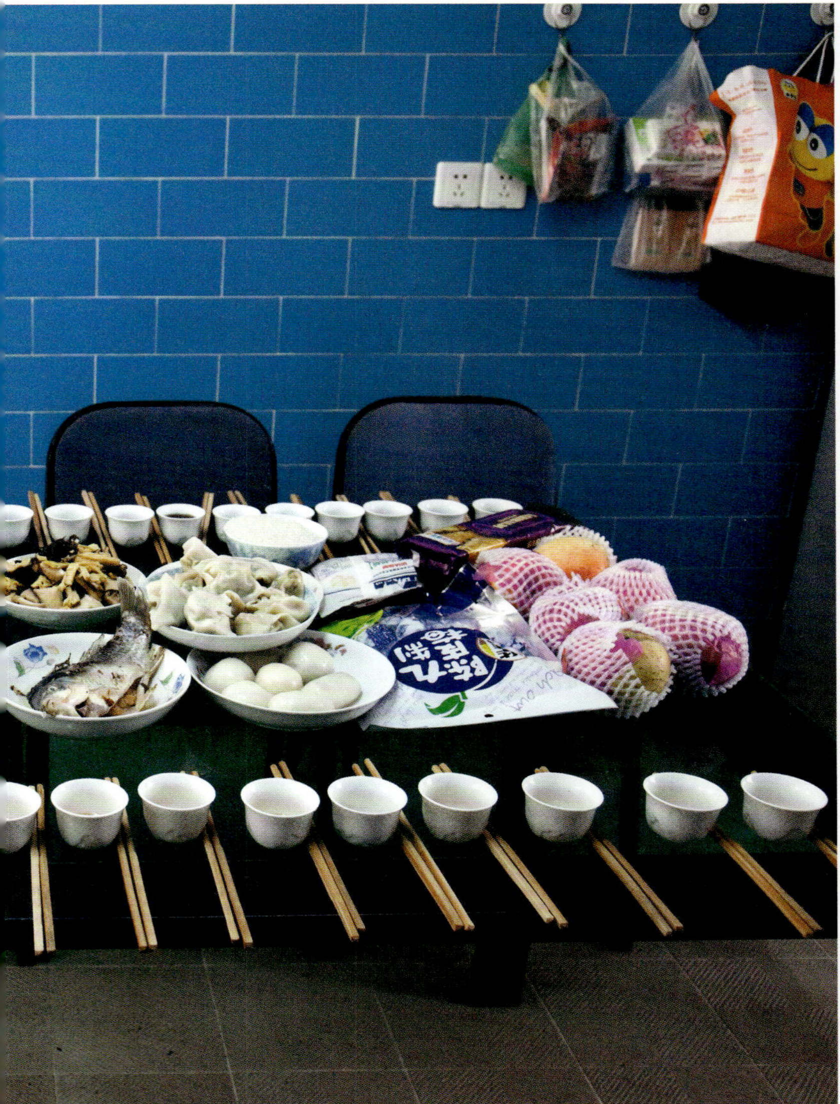

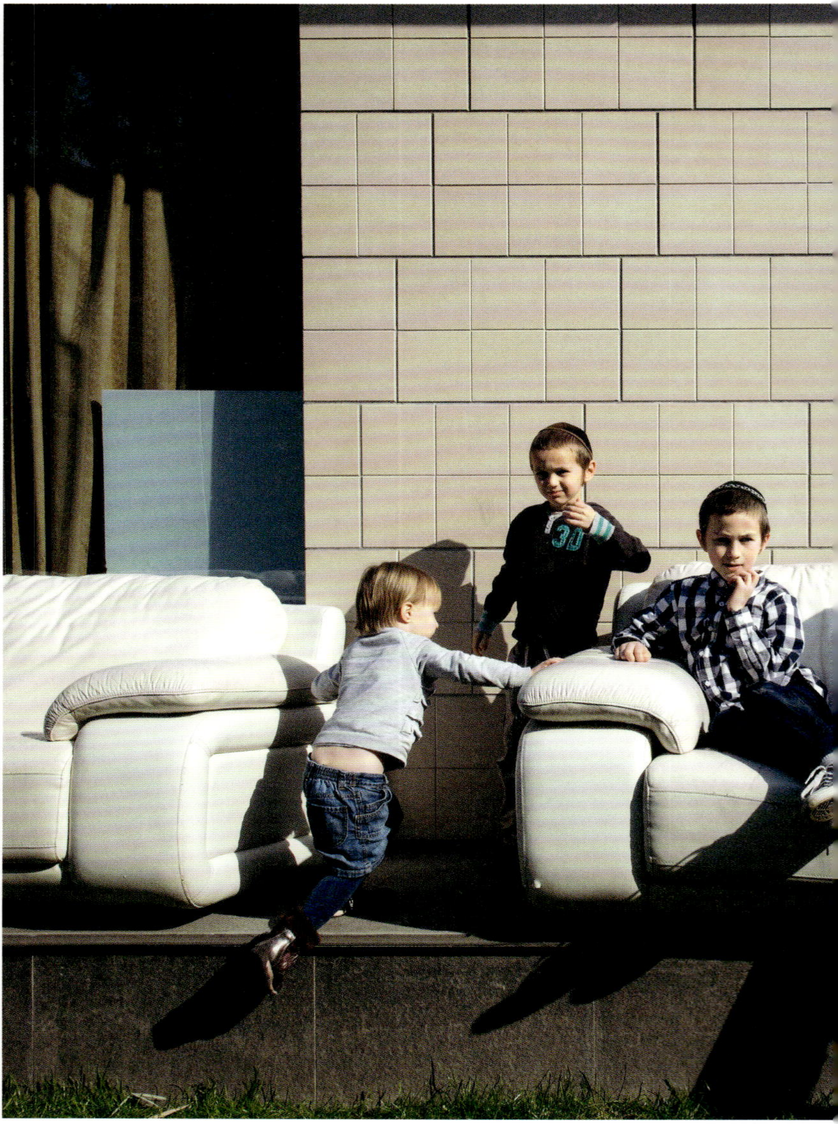

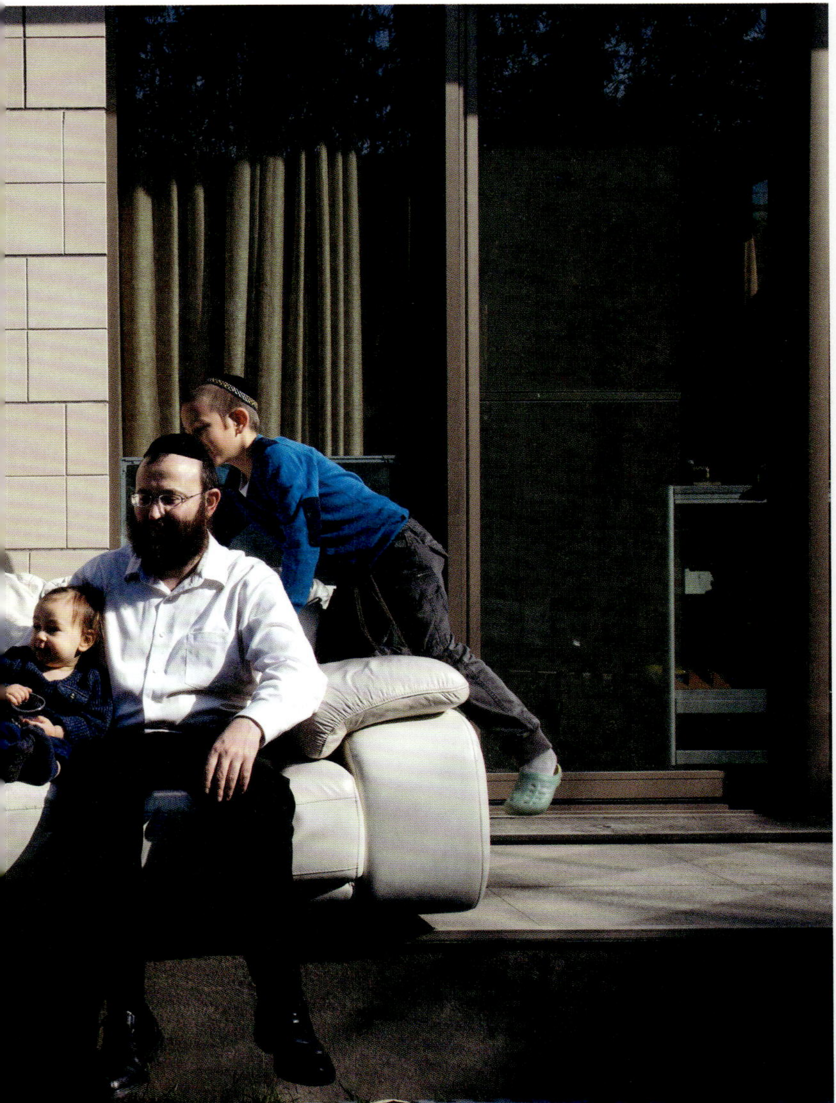

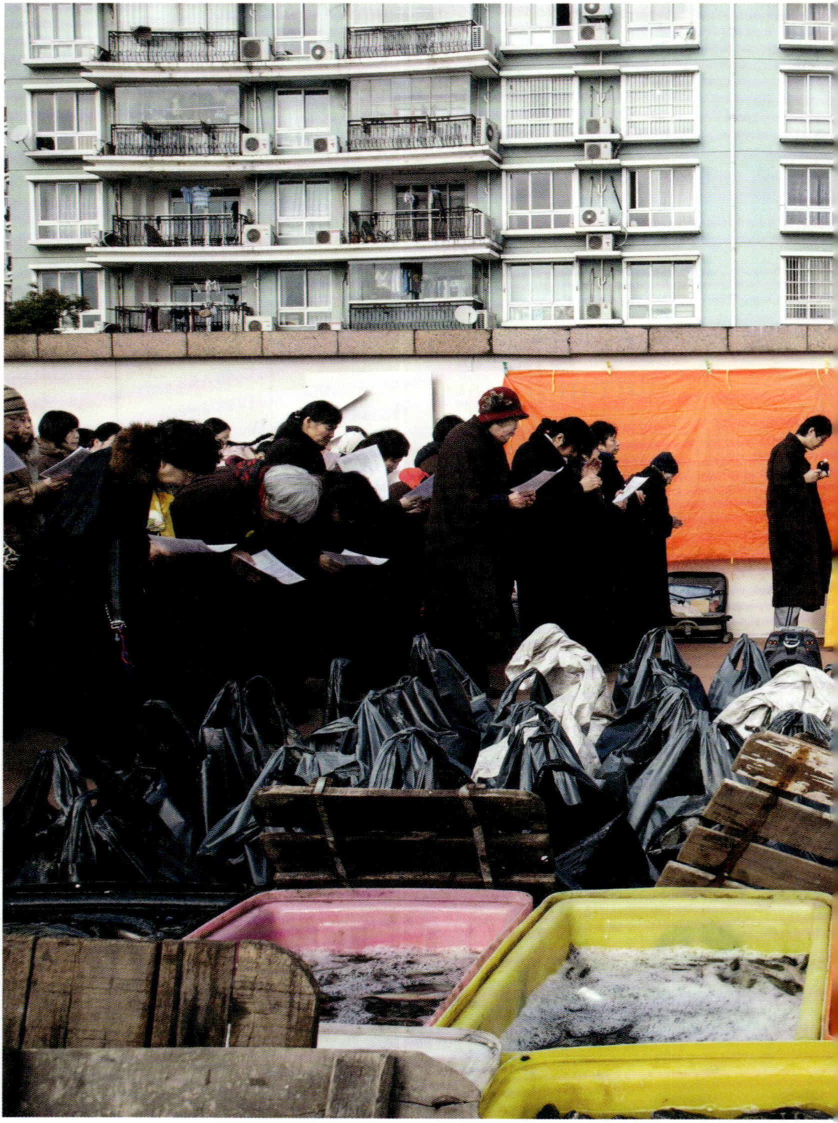

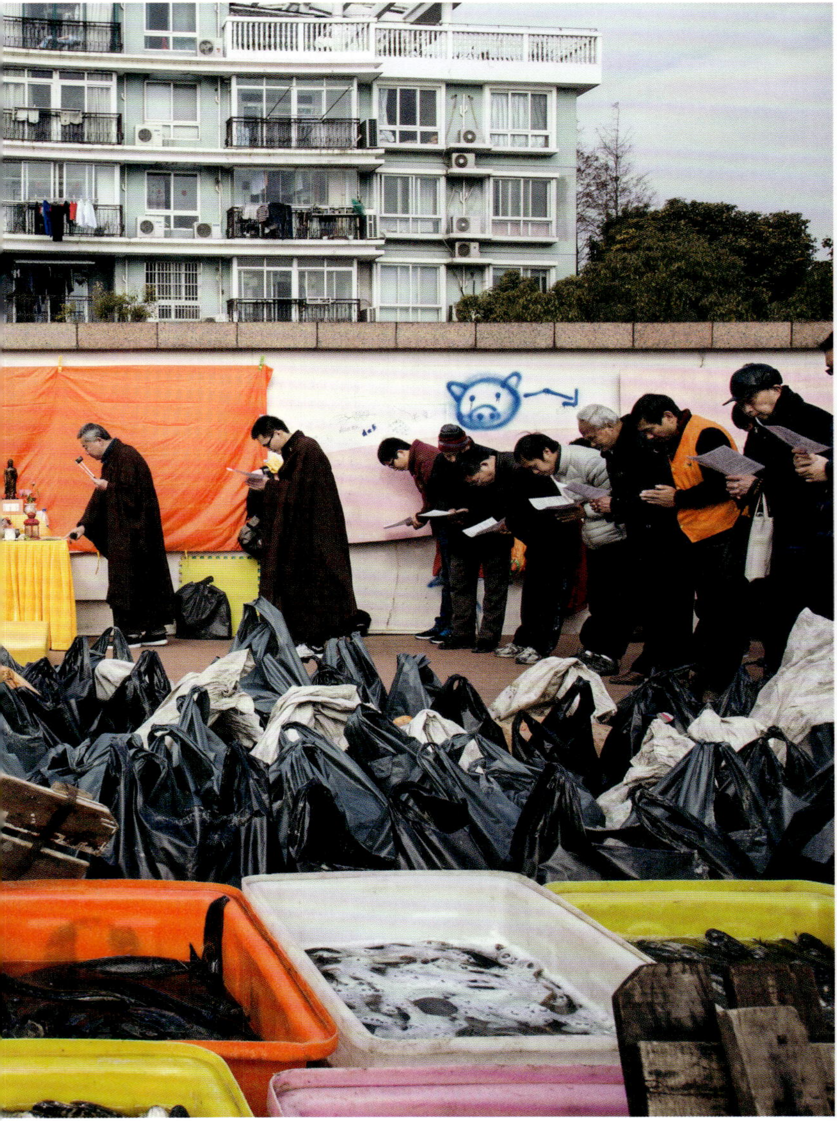

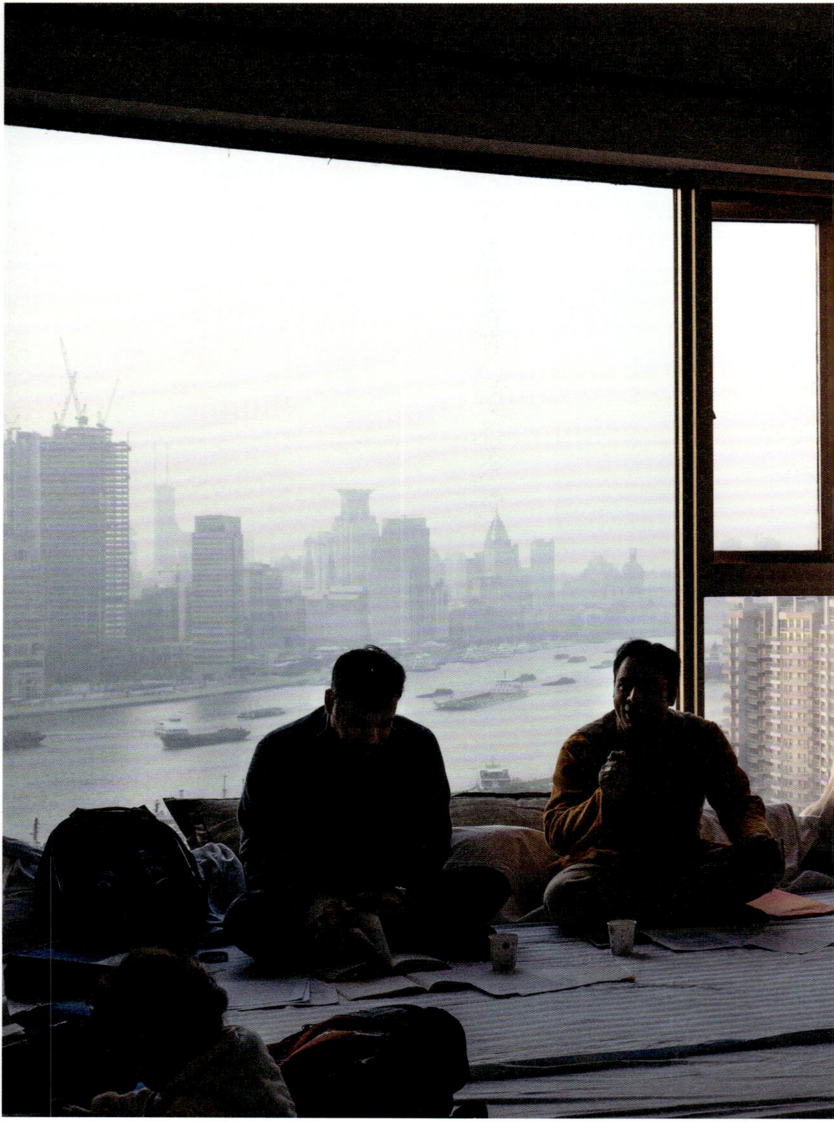

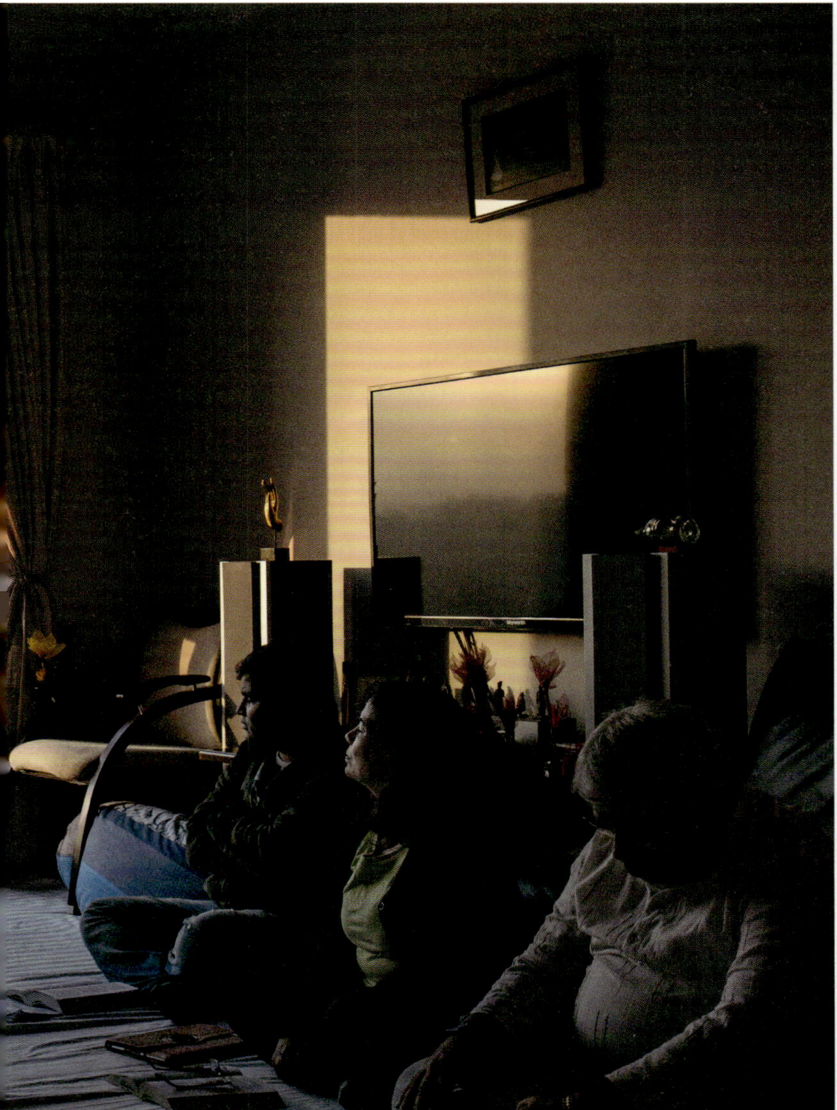

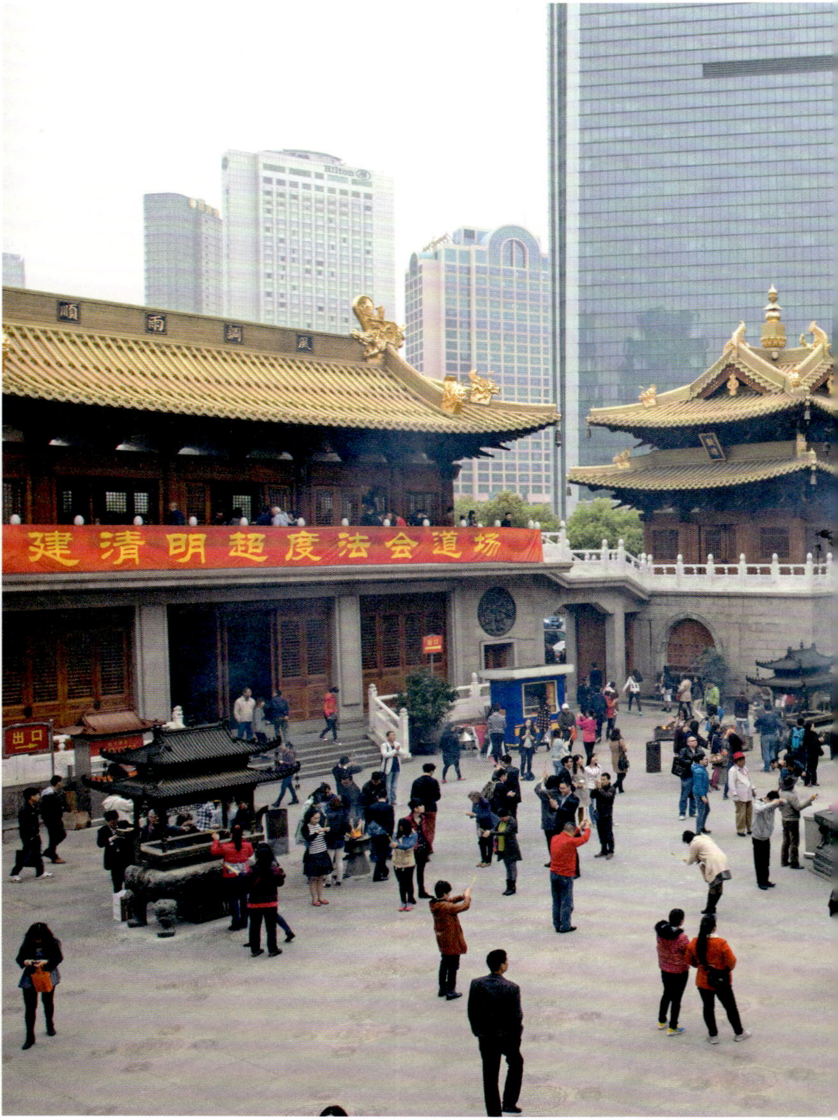
建清明超度法会道场
出口

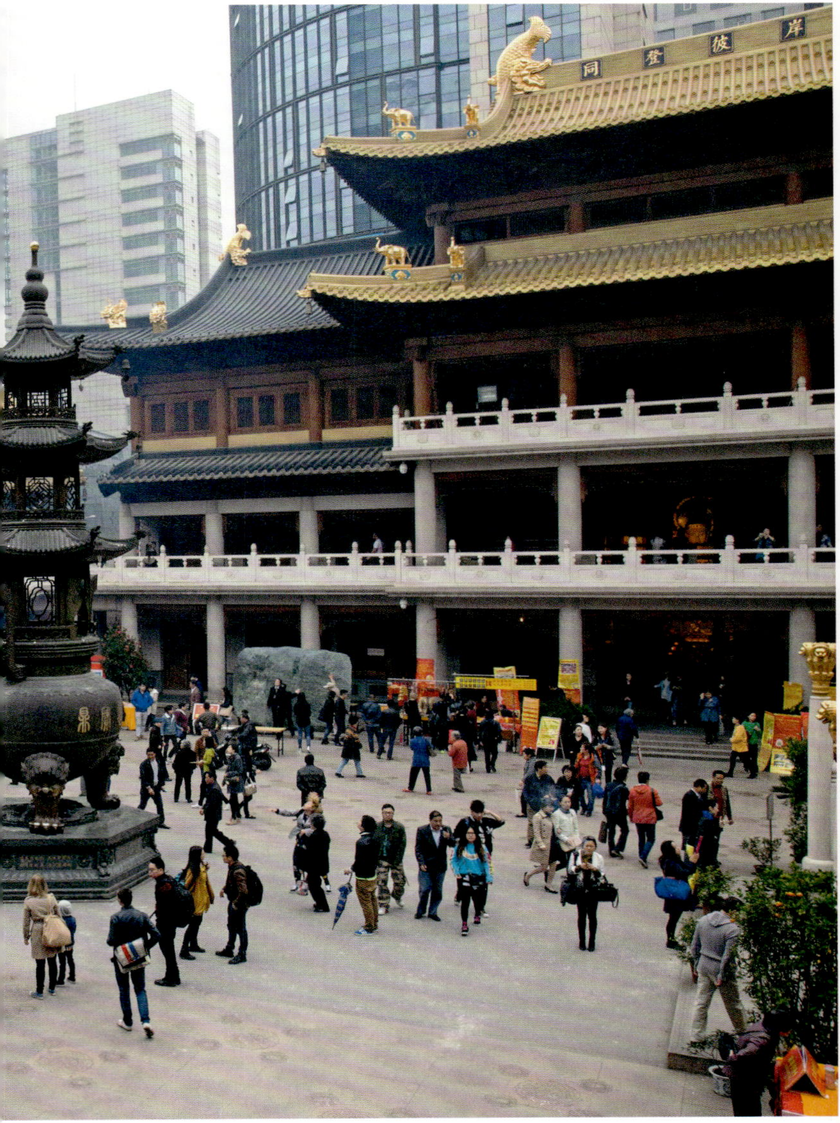
同登彼岸

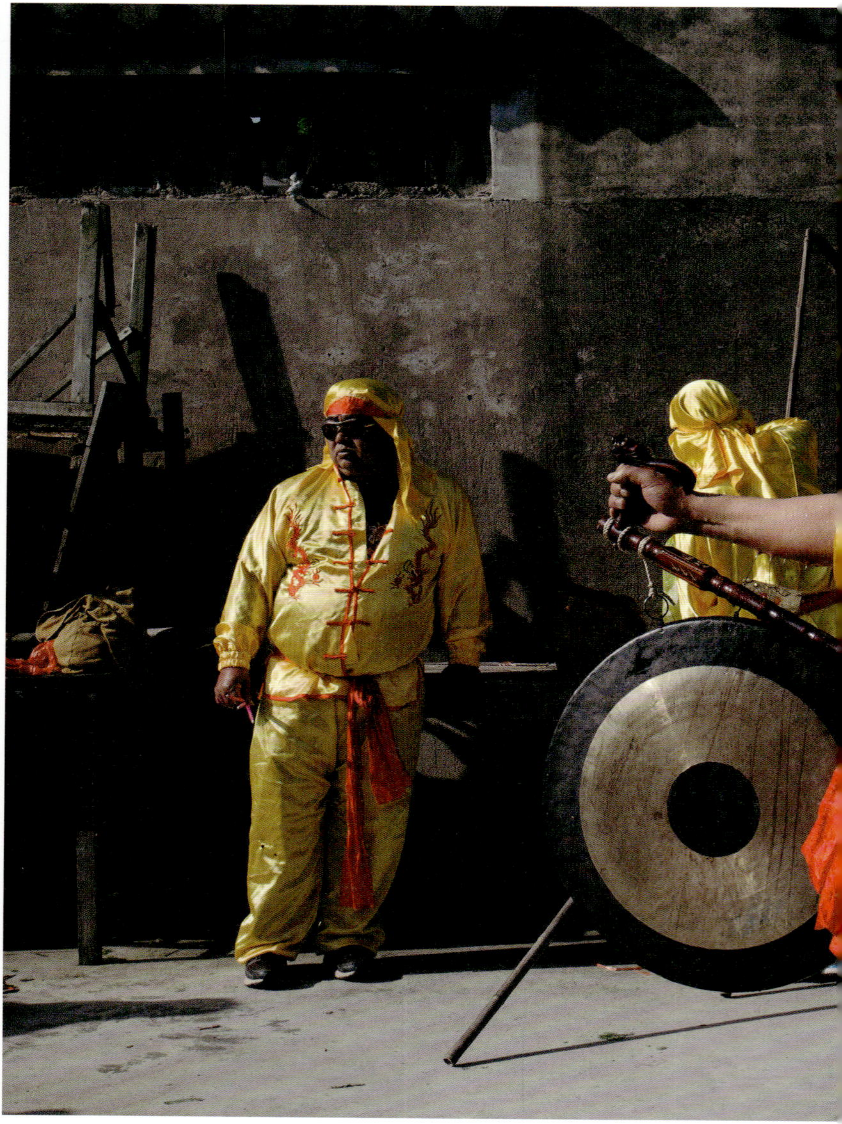

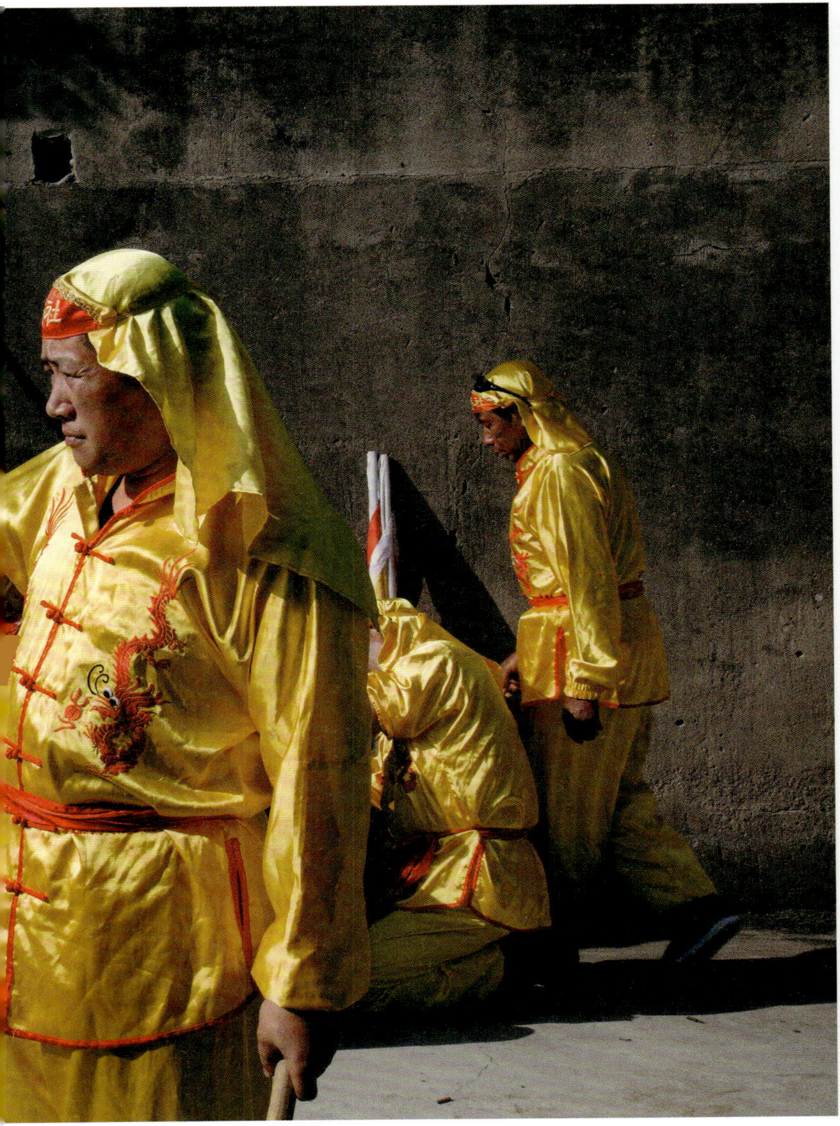

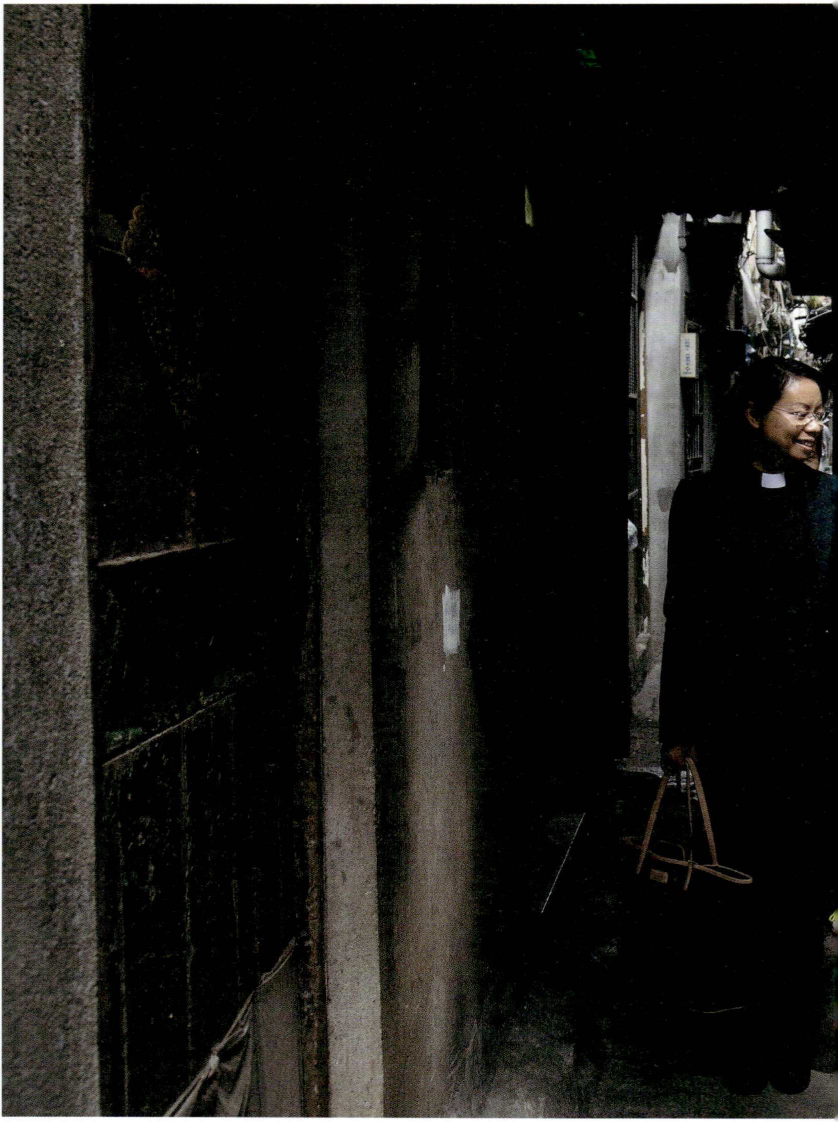

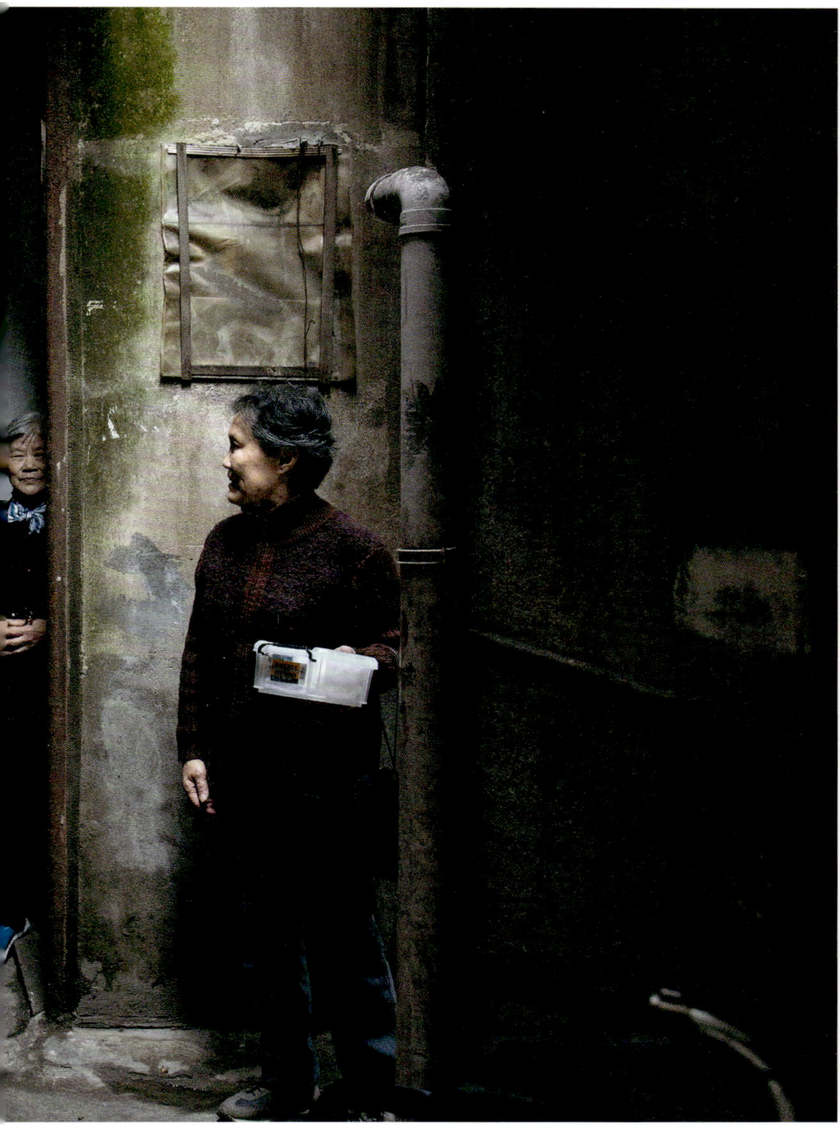

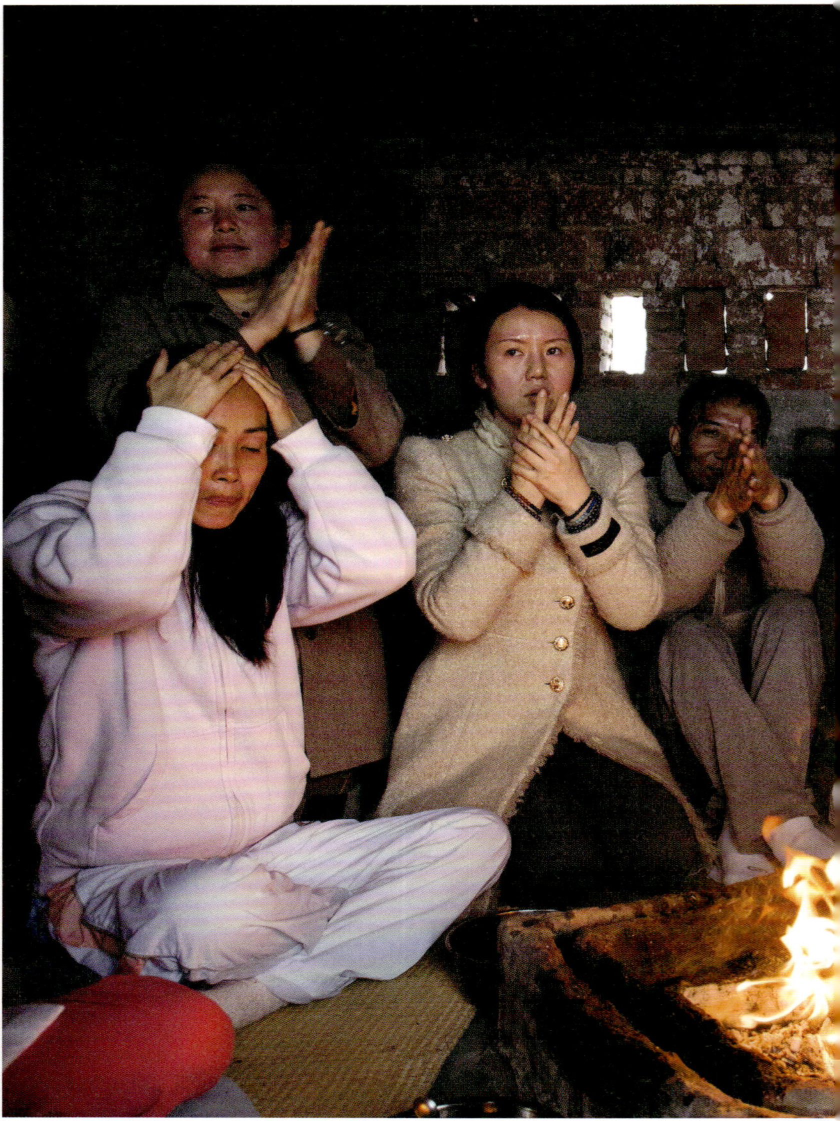

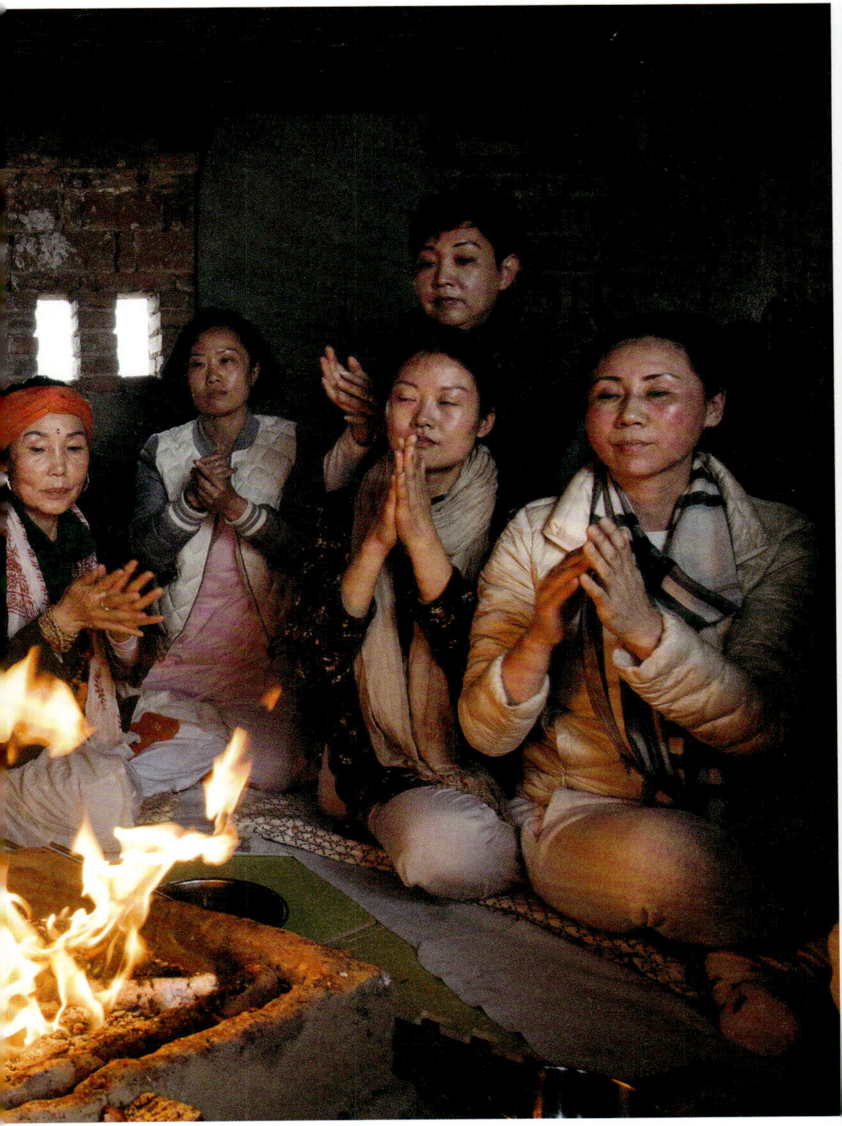

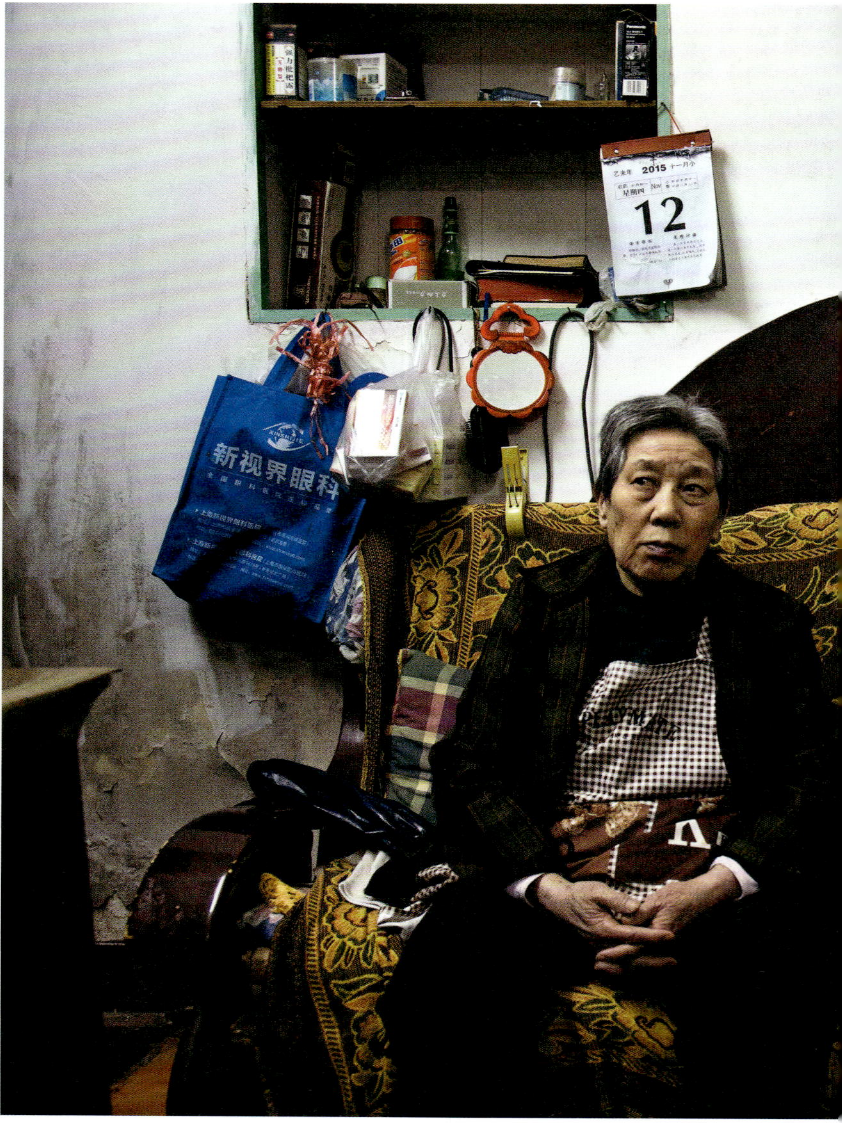
乙未年 2015 十一月小
星期四
Nov
12
新视界眼科

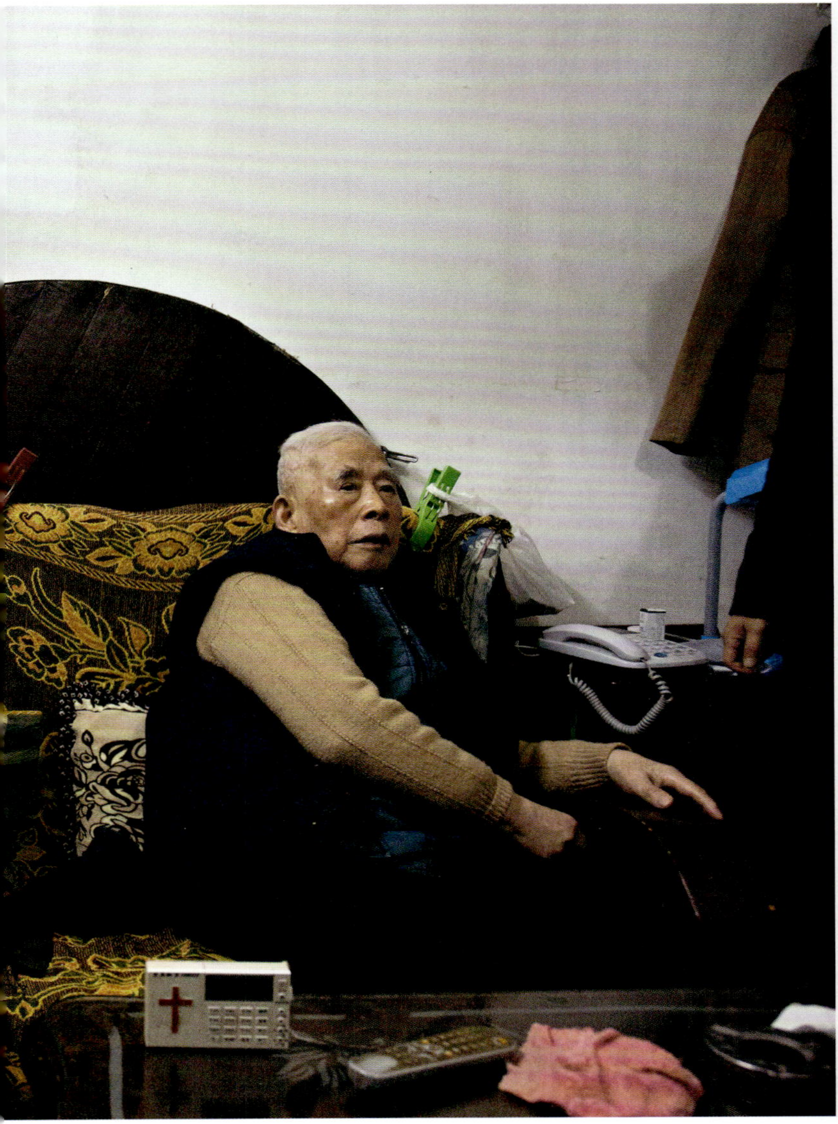

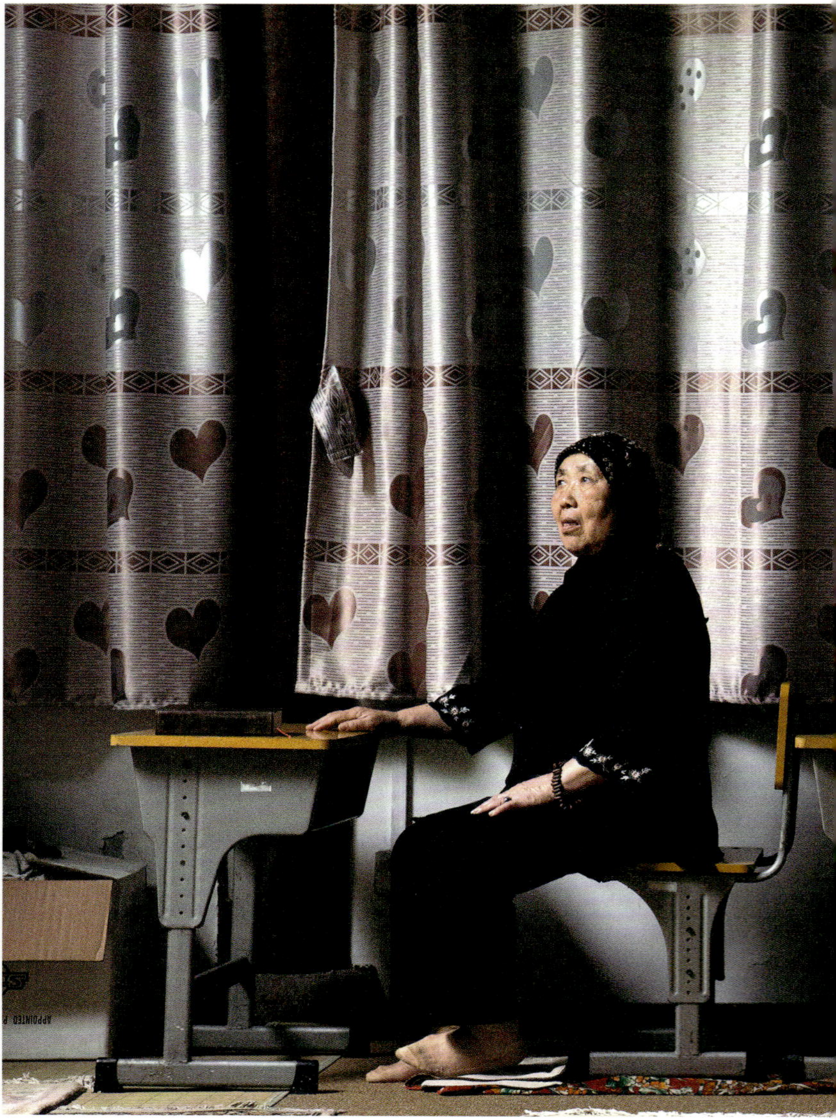

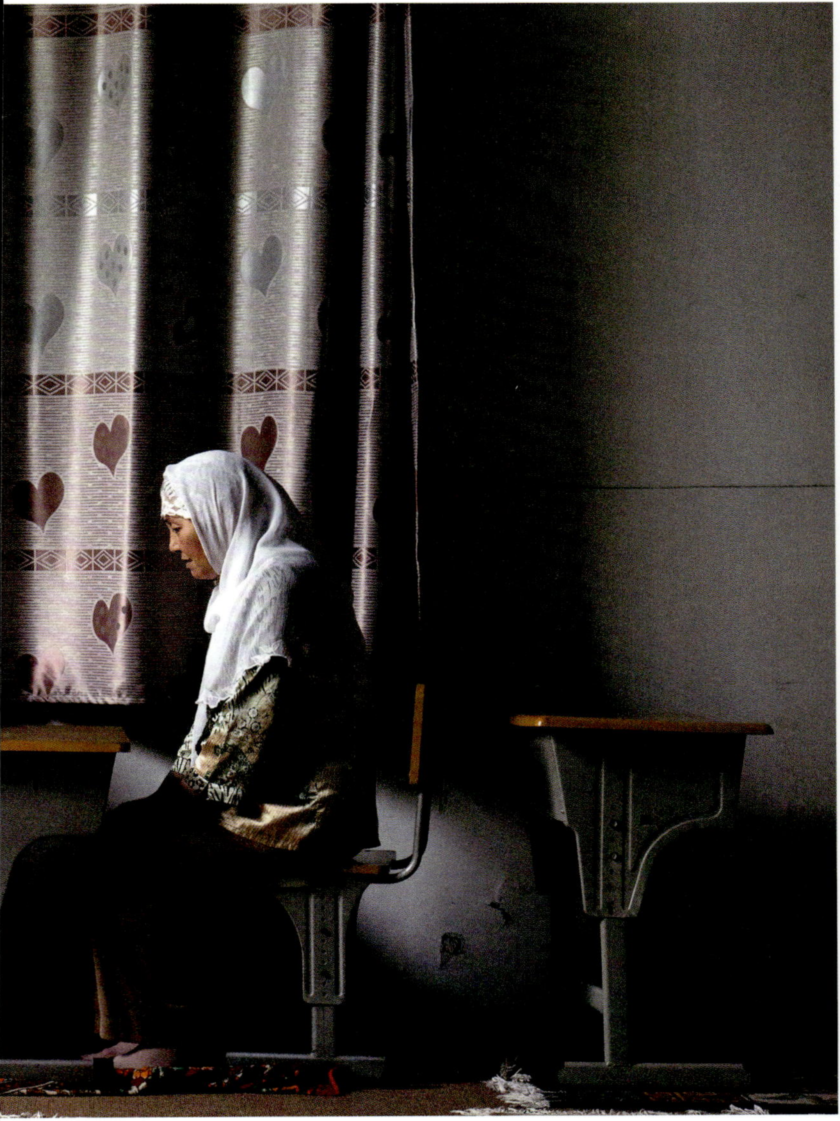

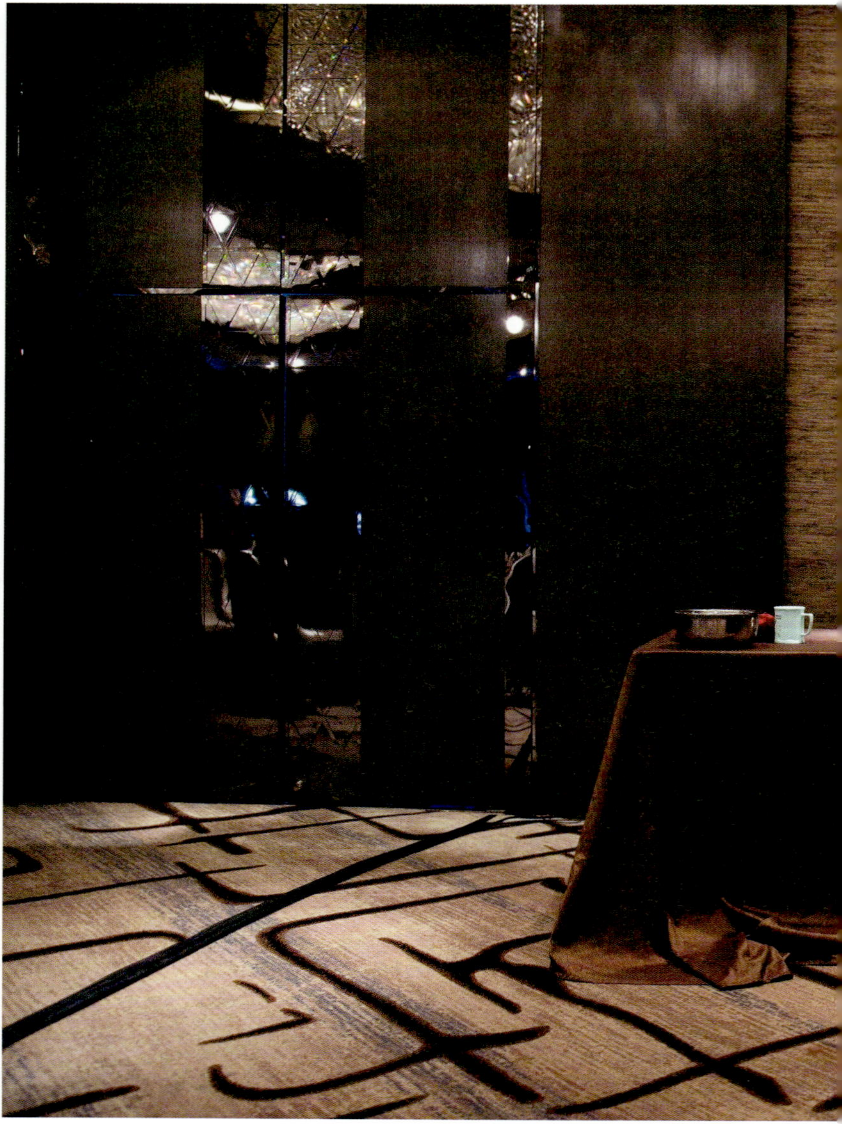

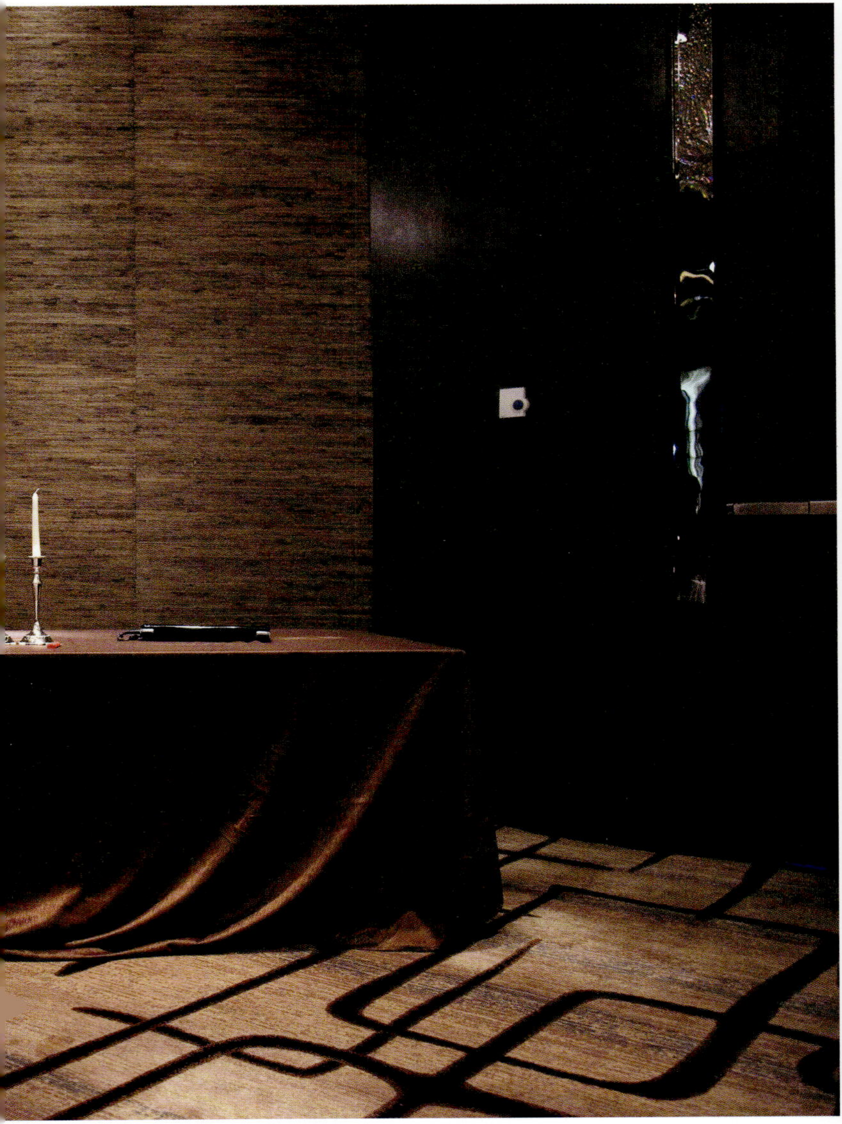

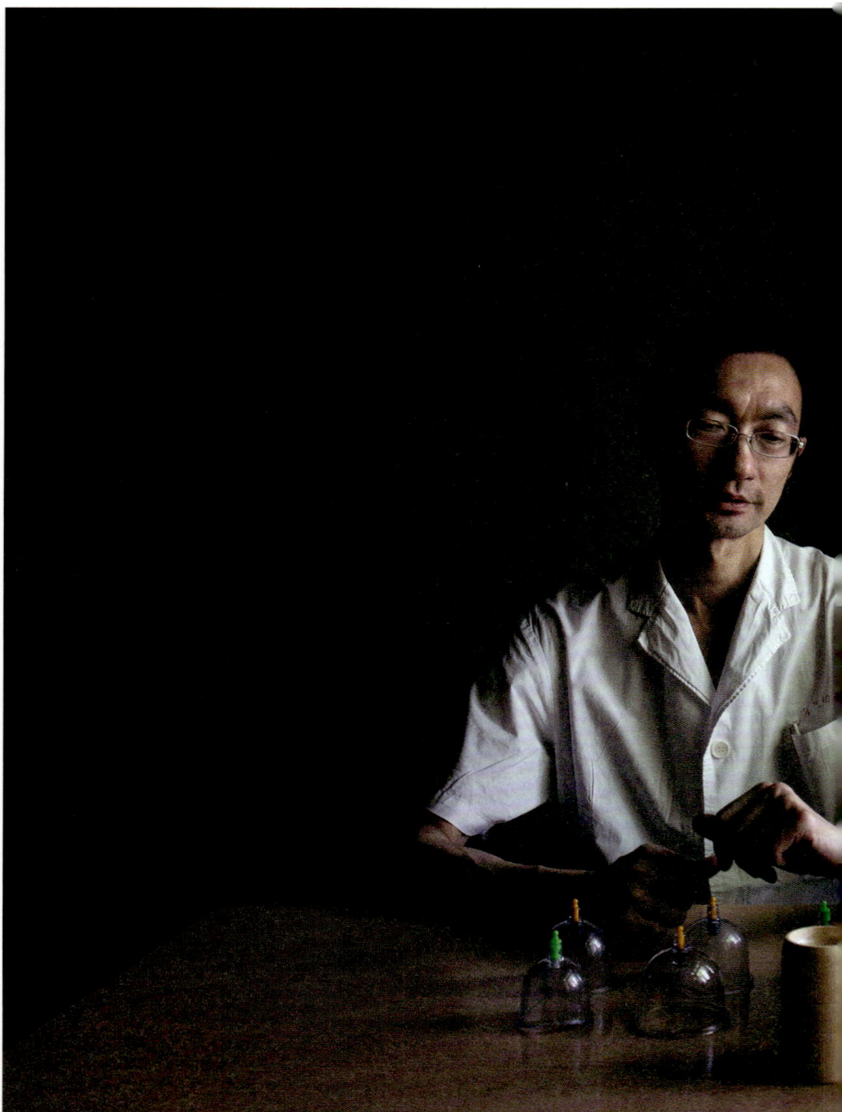

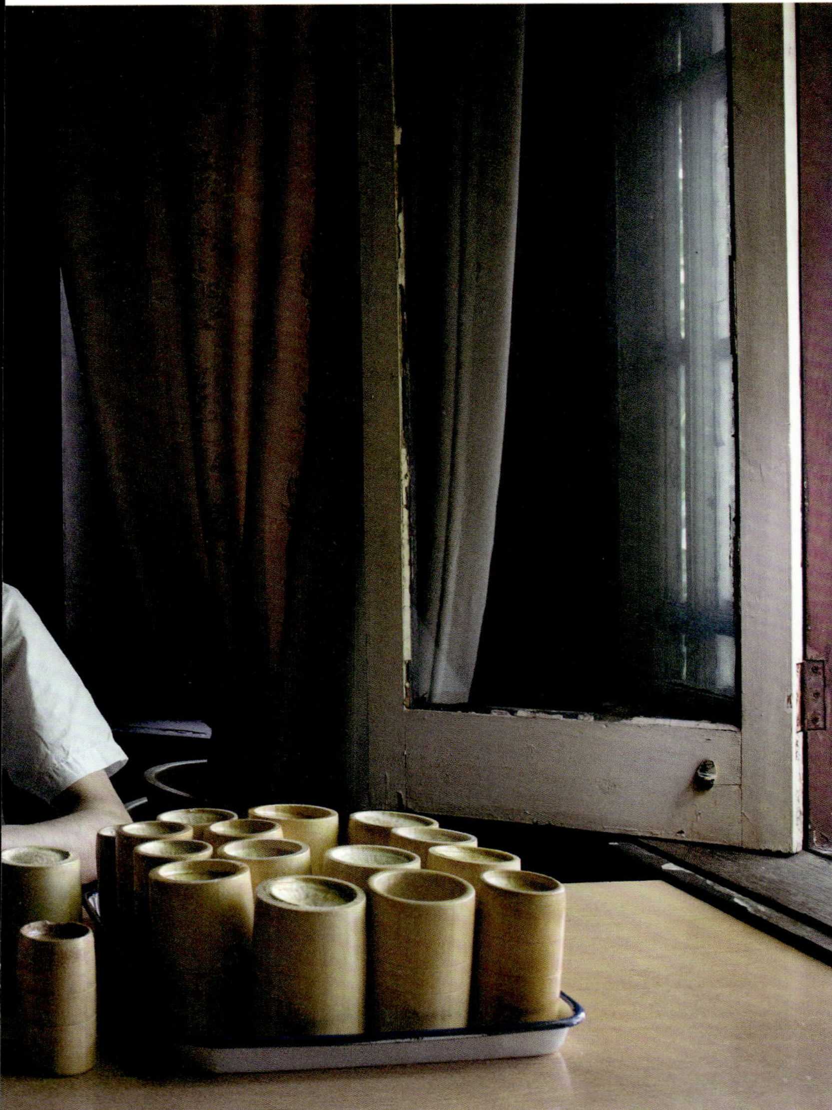

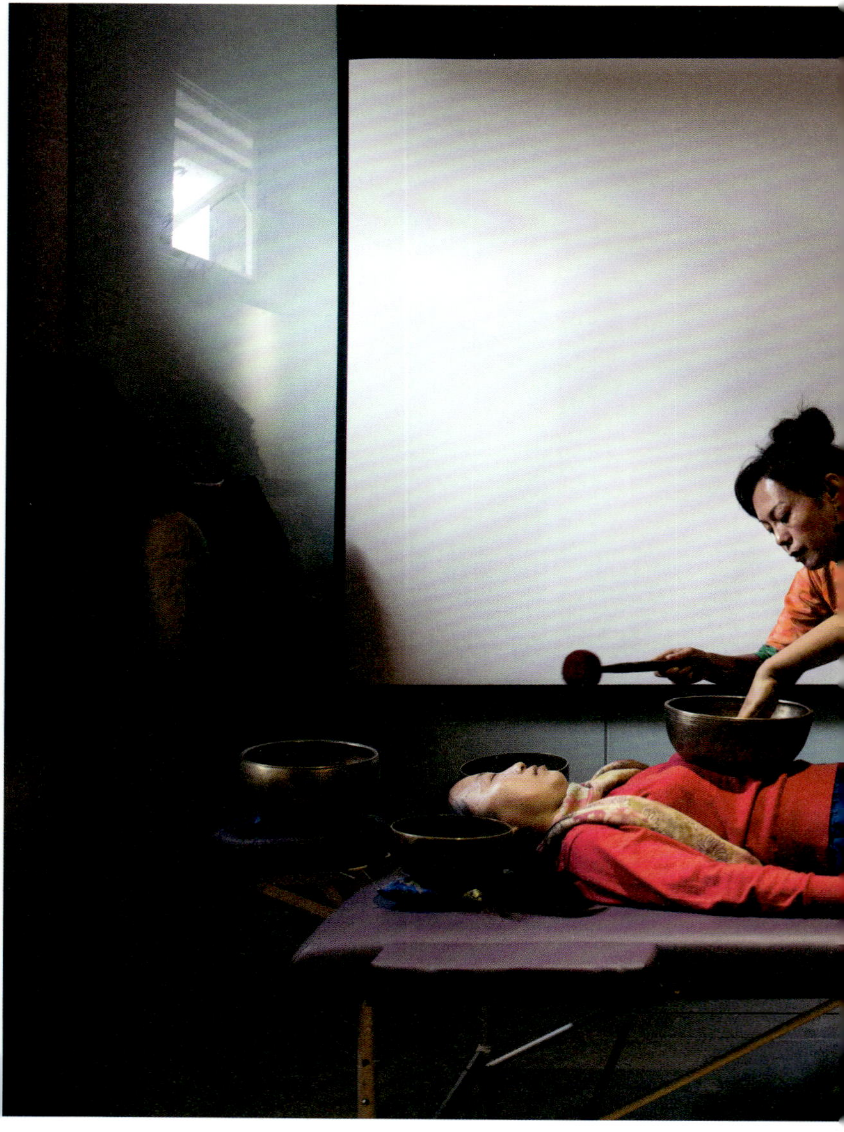

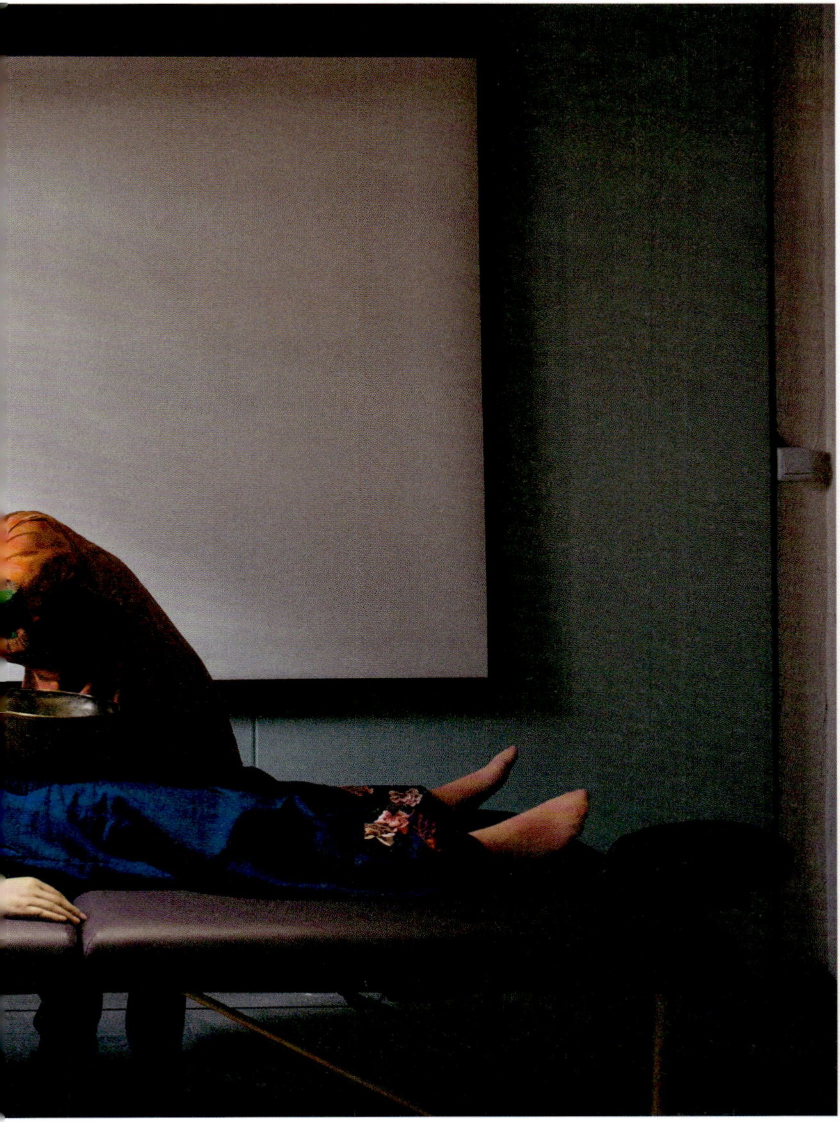

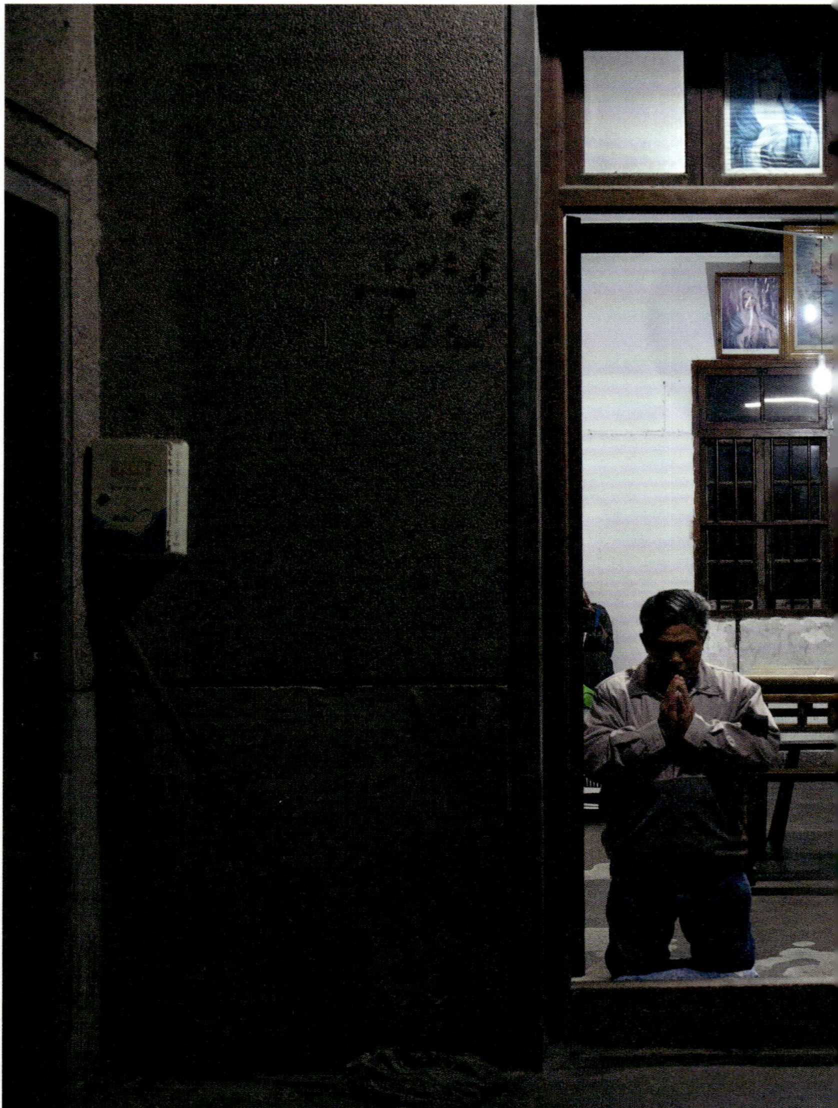

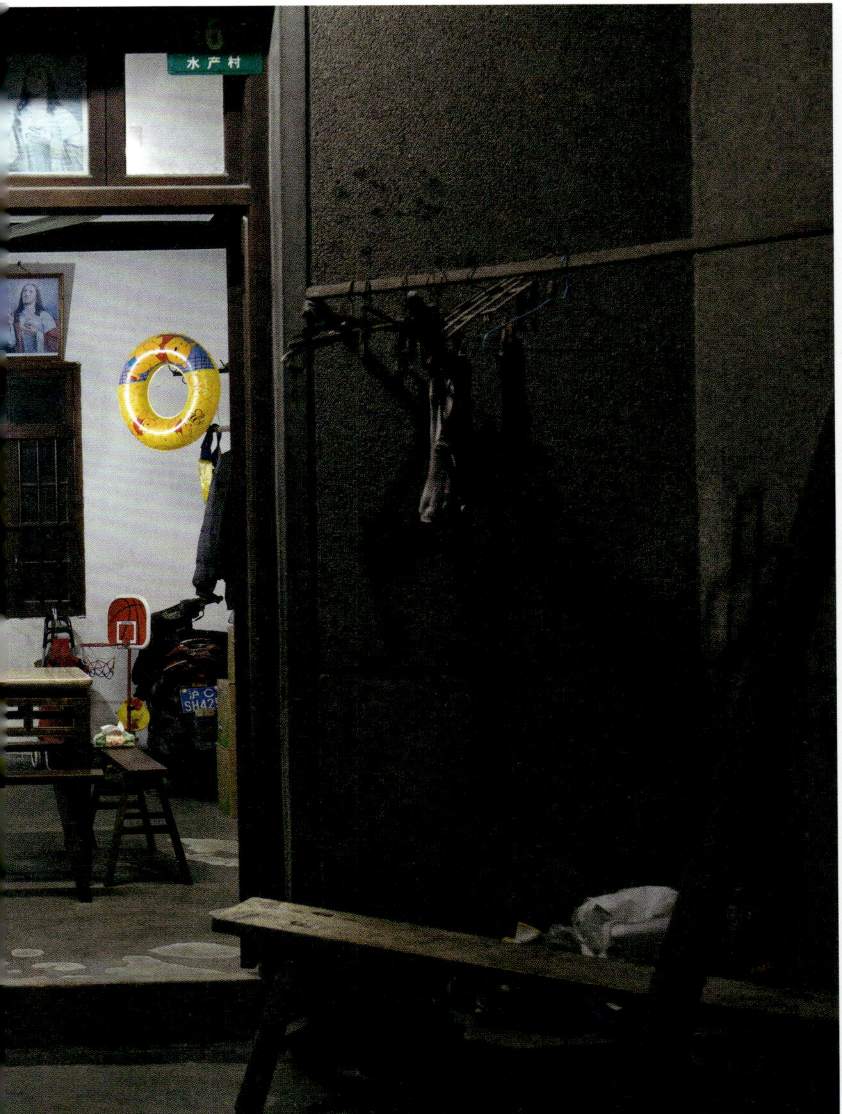
水产村

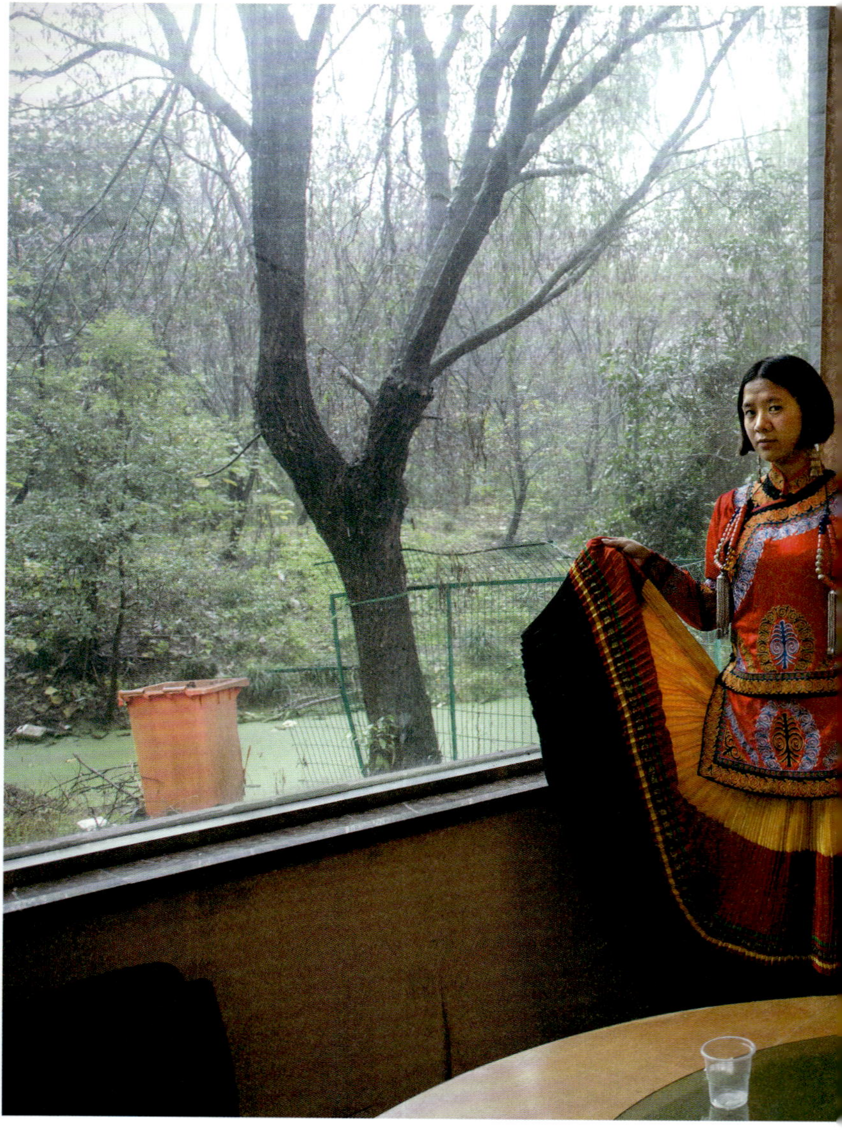

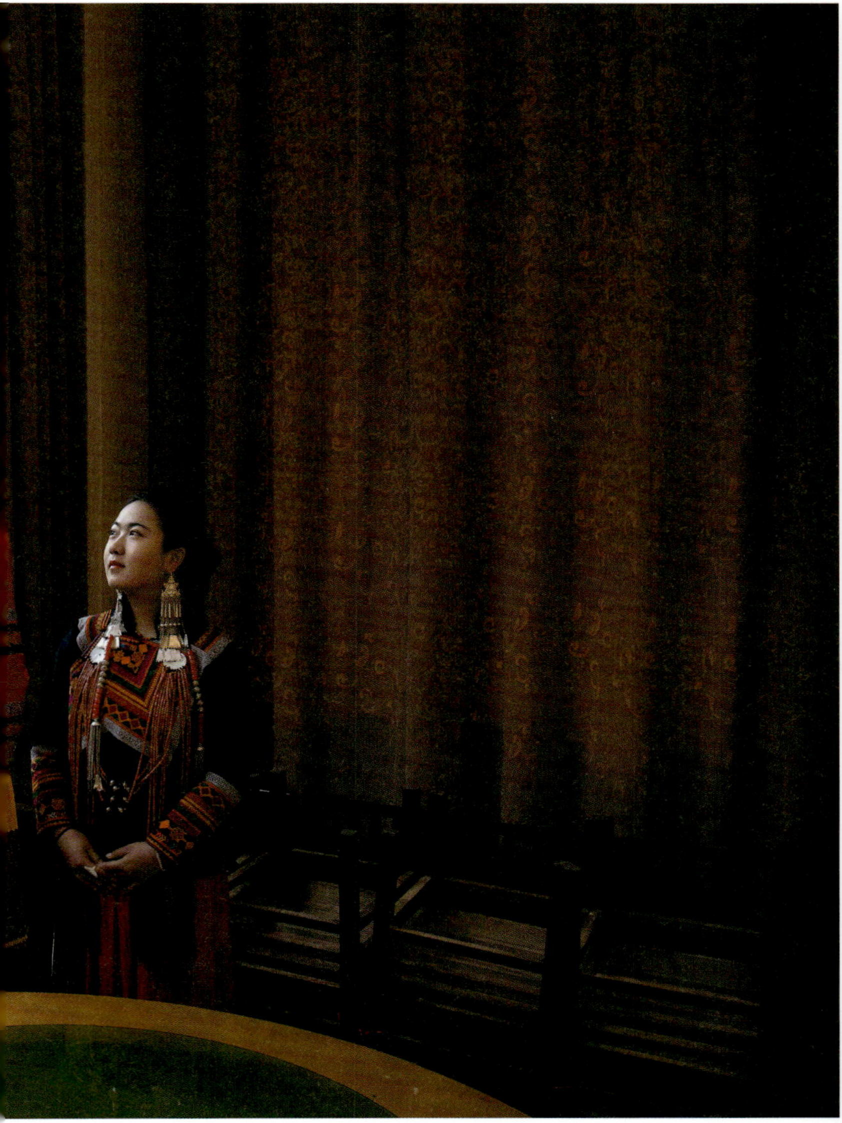

39

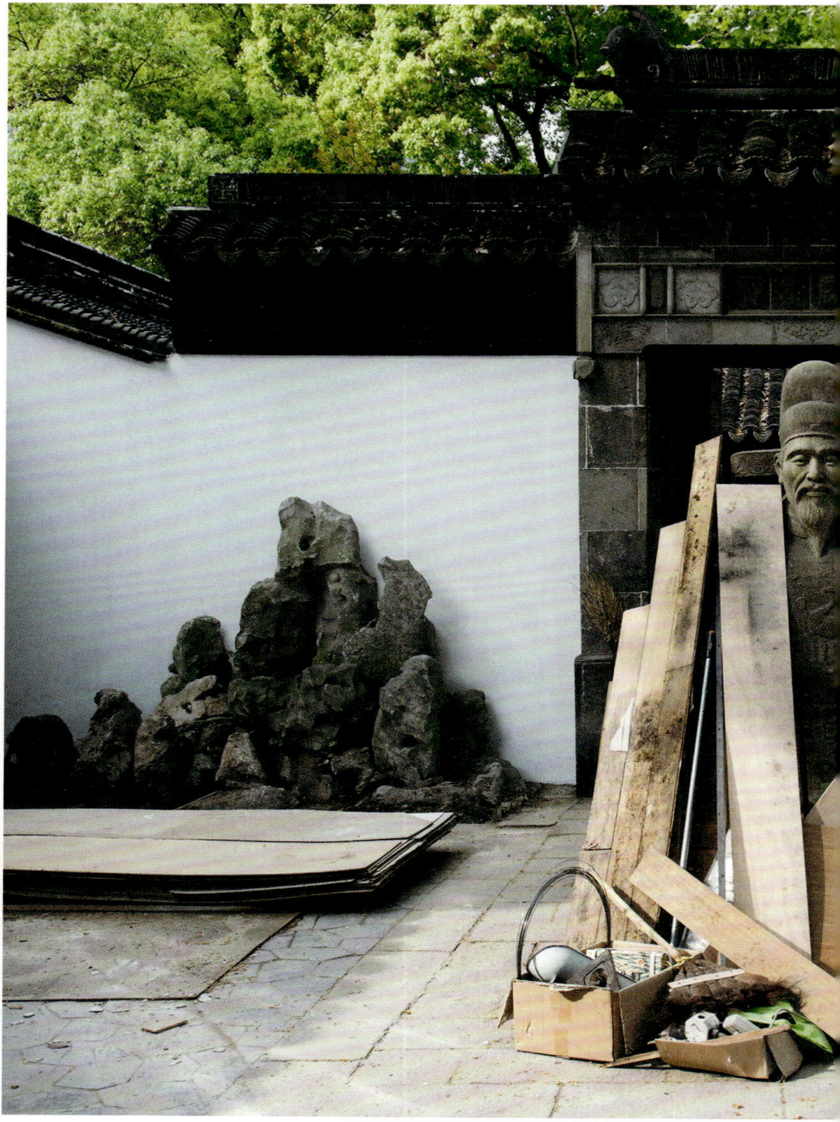

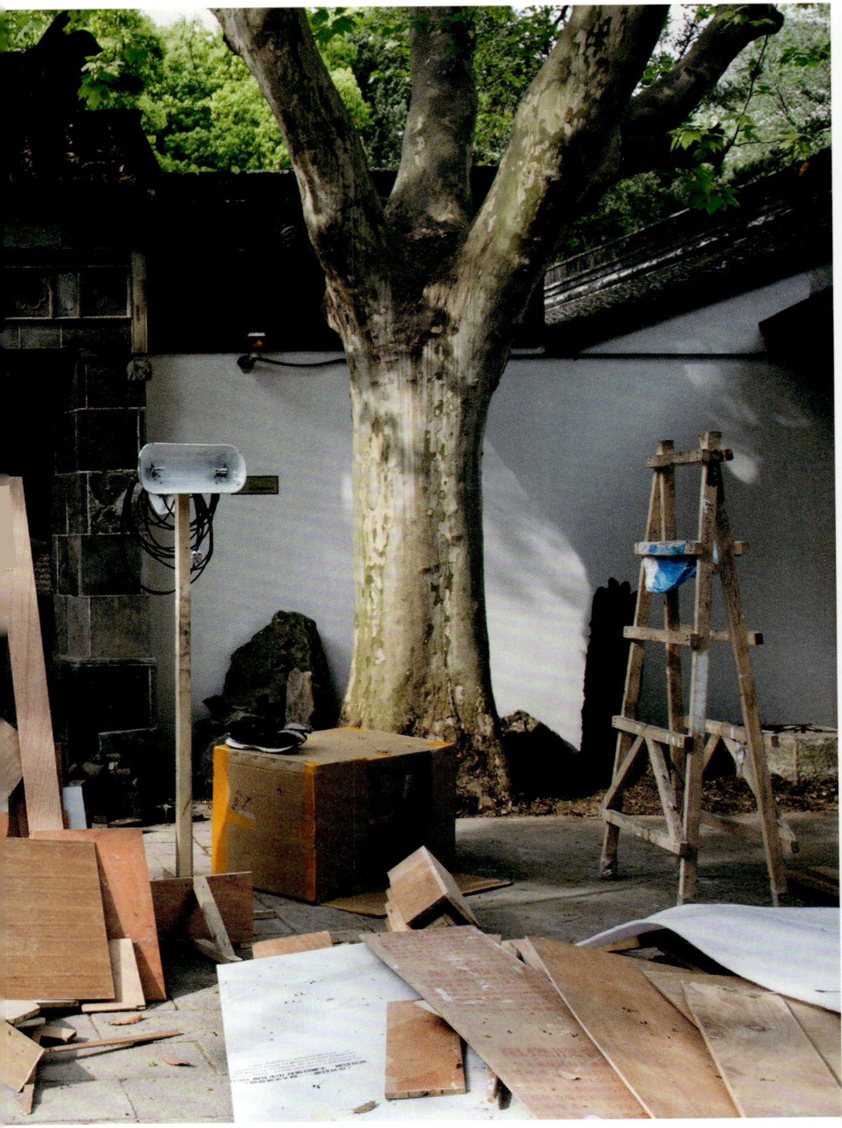

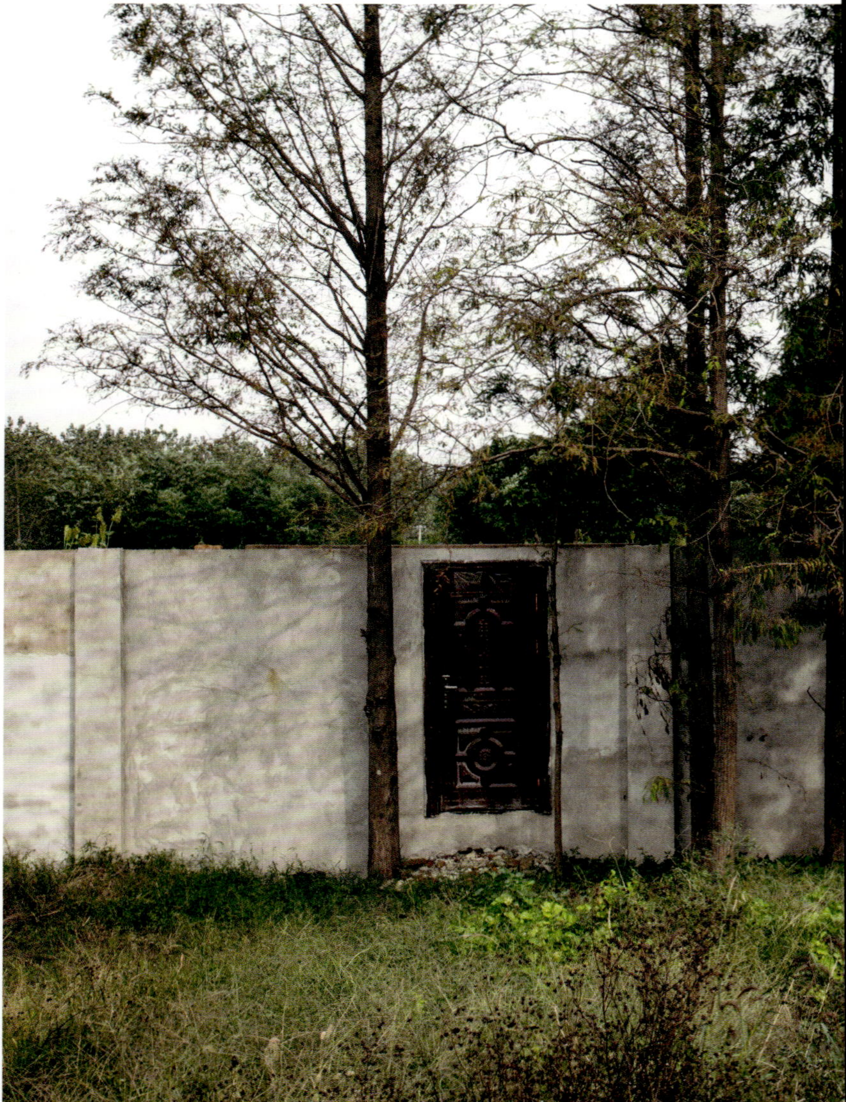

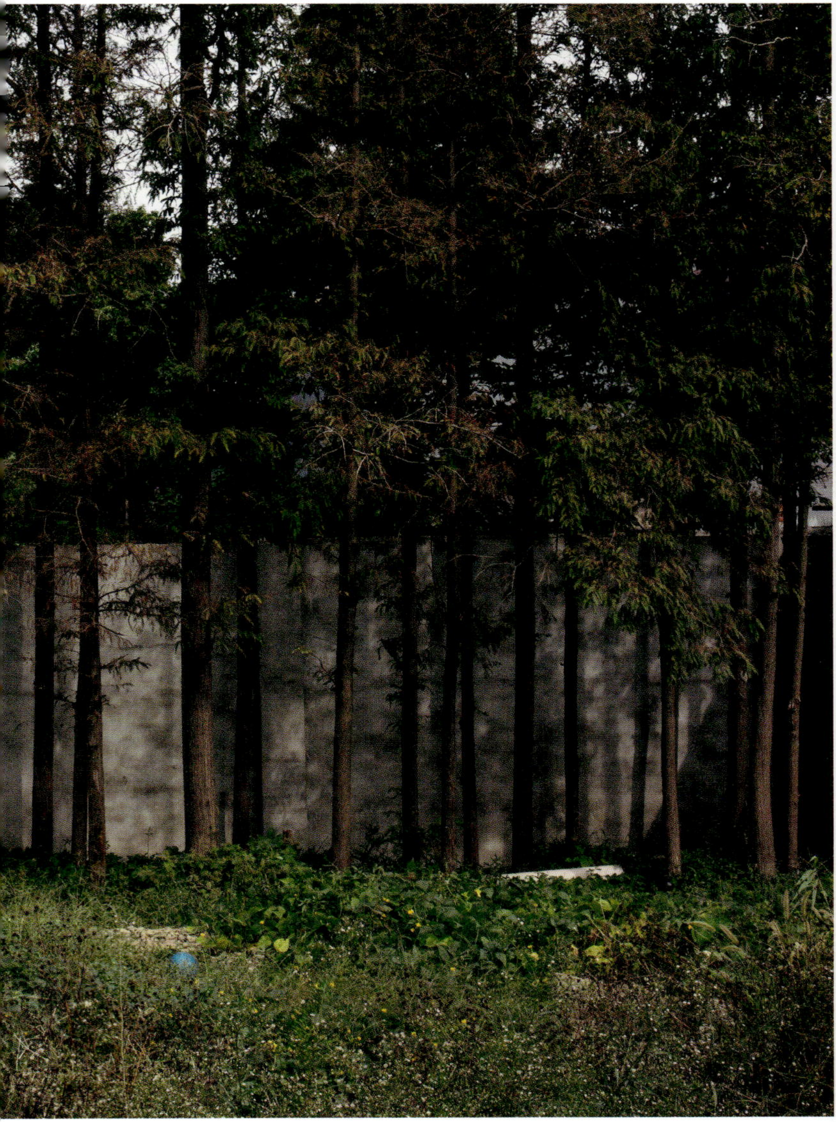

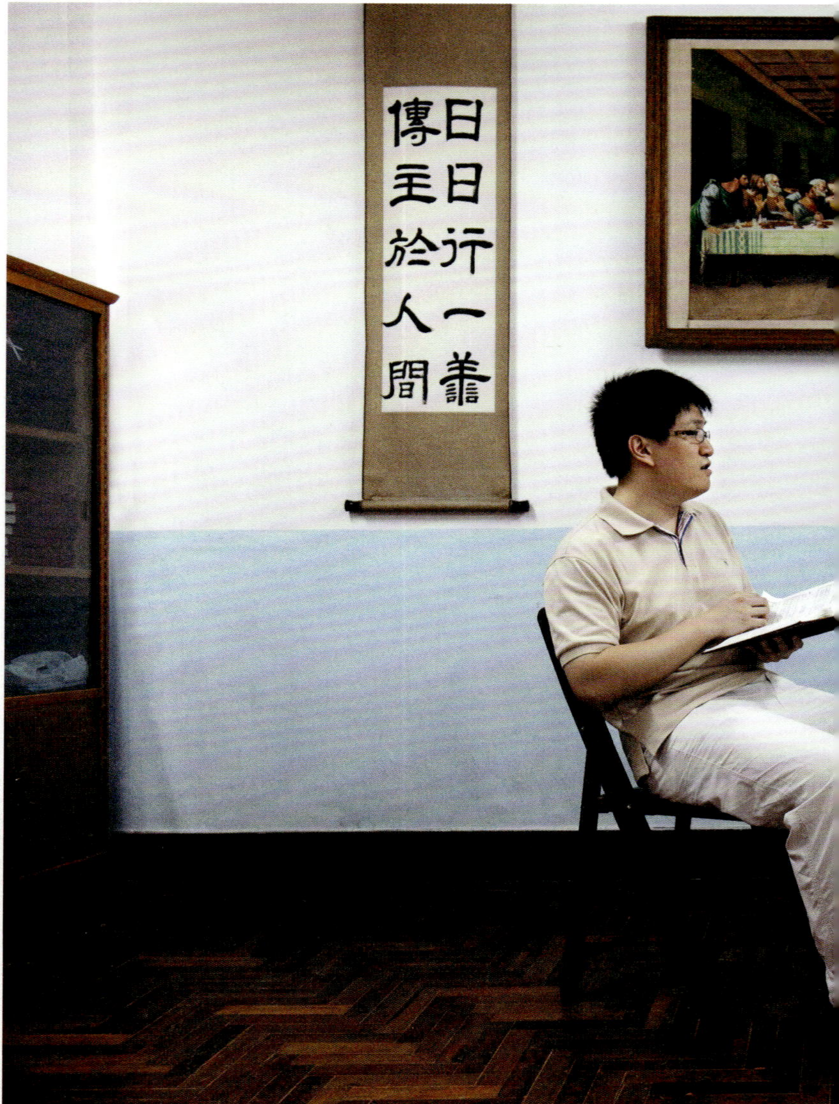
日日行一善
傳主於人間

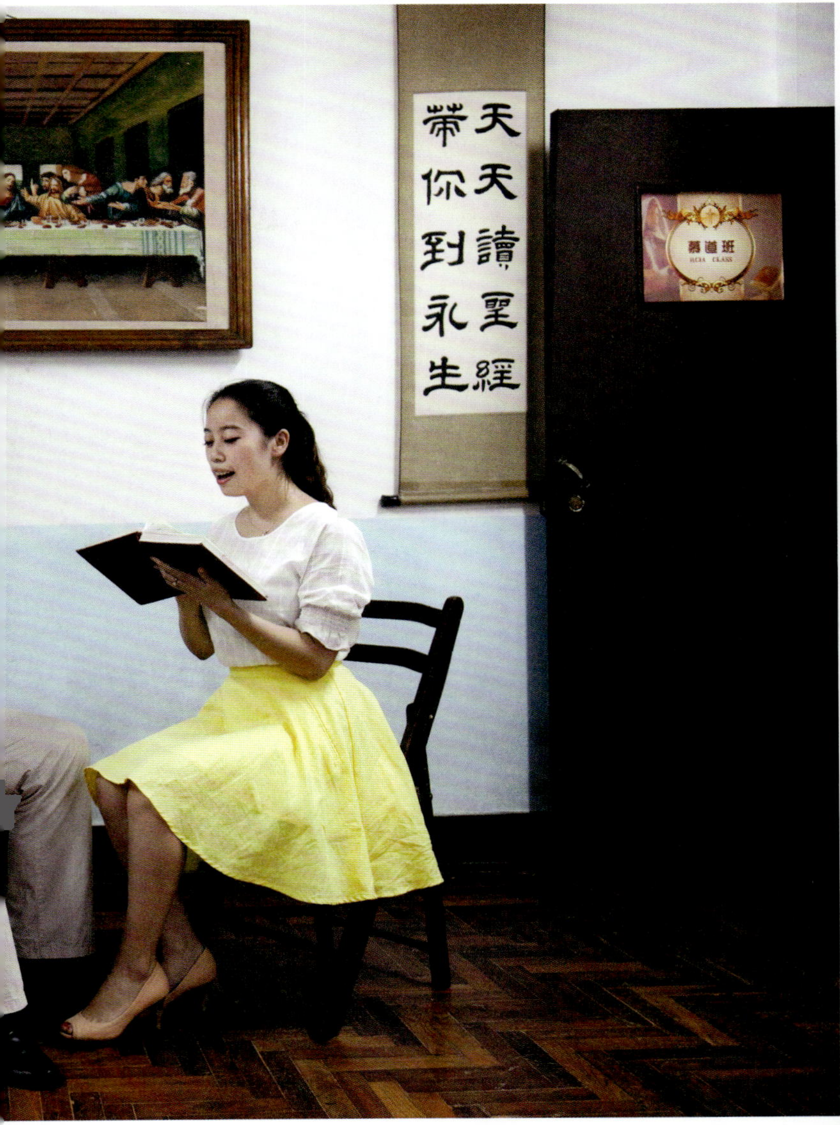
天天讀聖經
帶你到永生

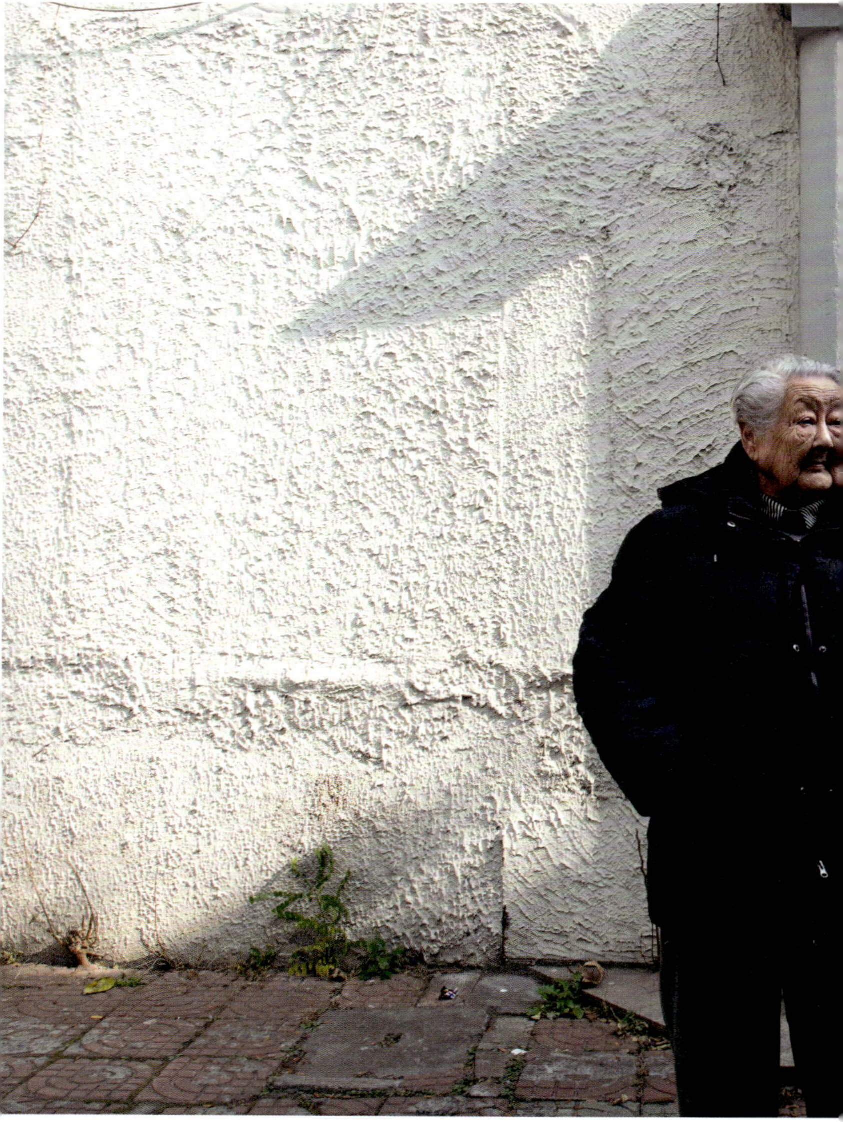

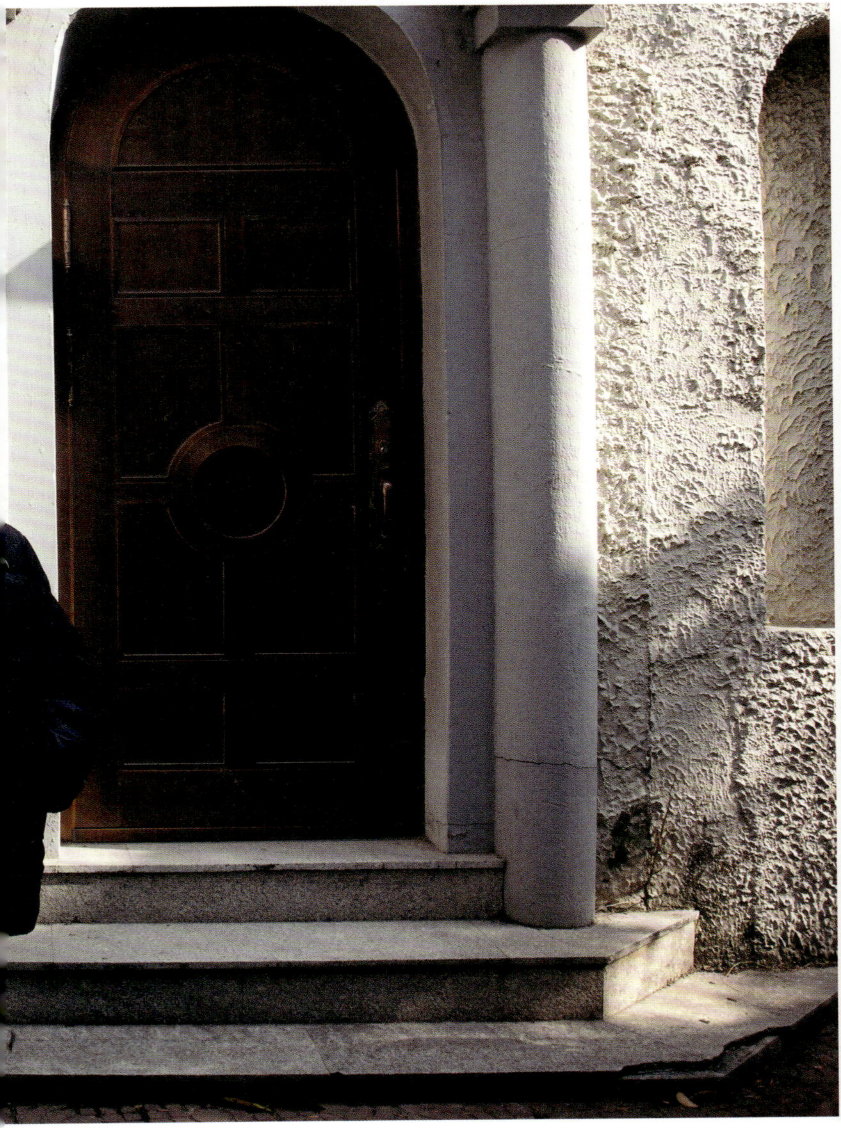

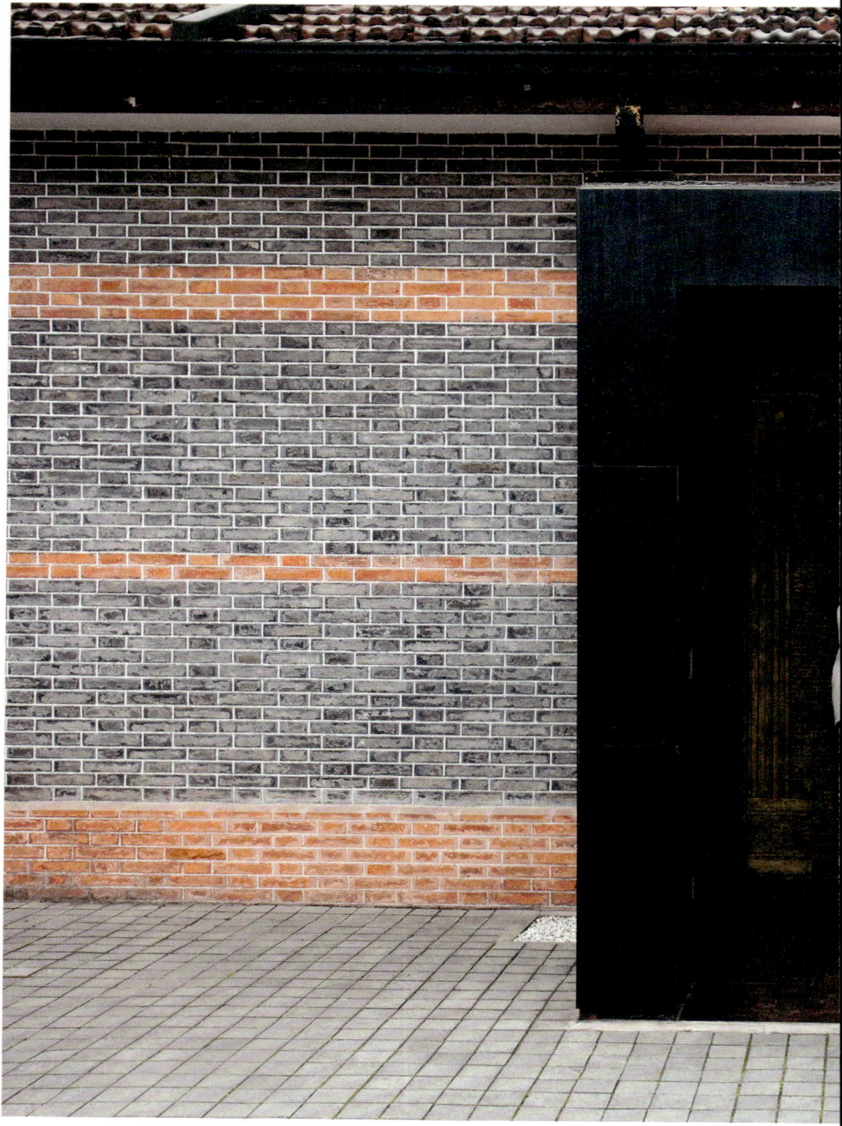

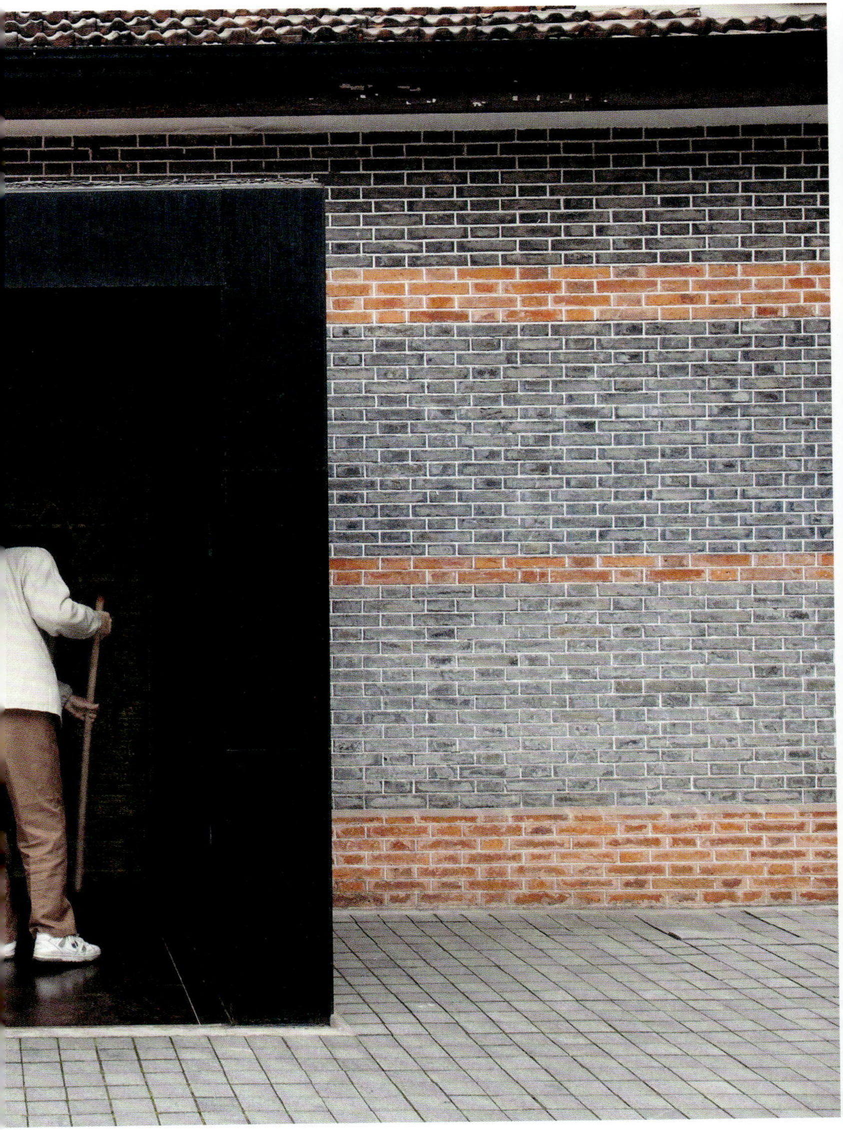

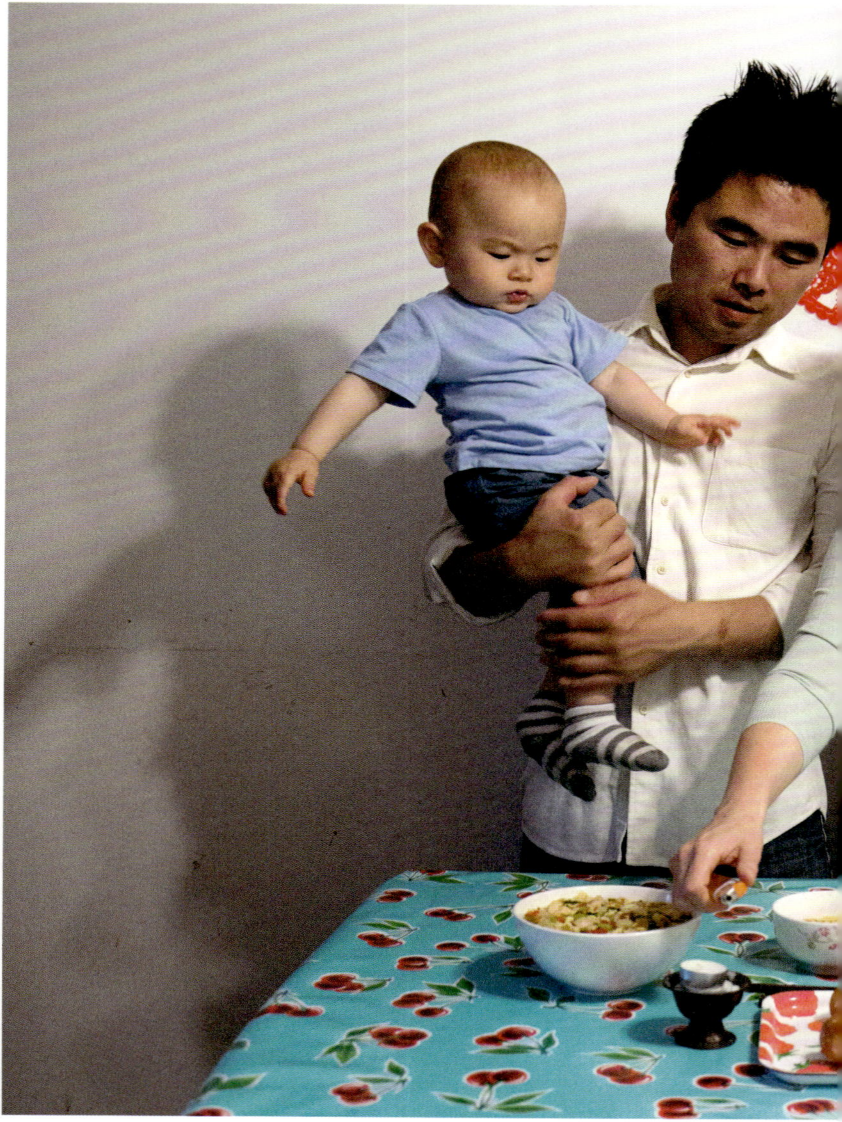

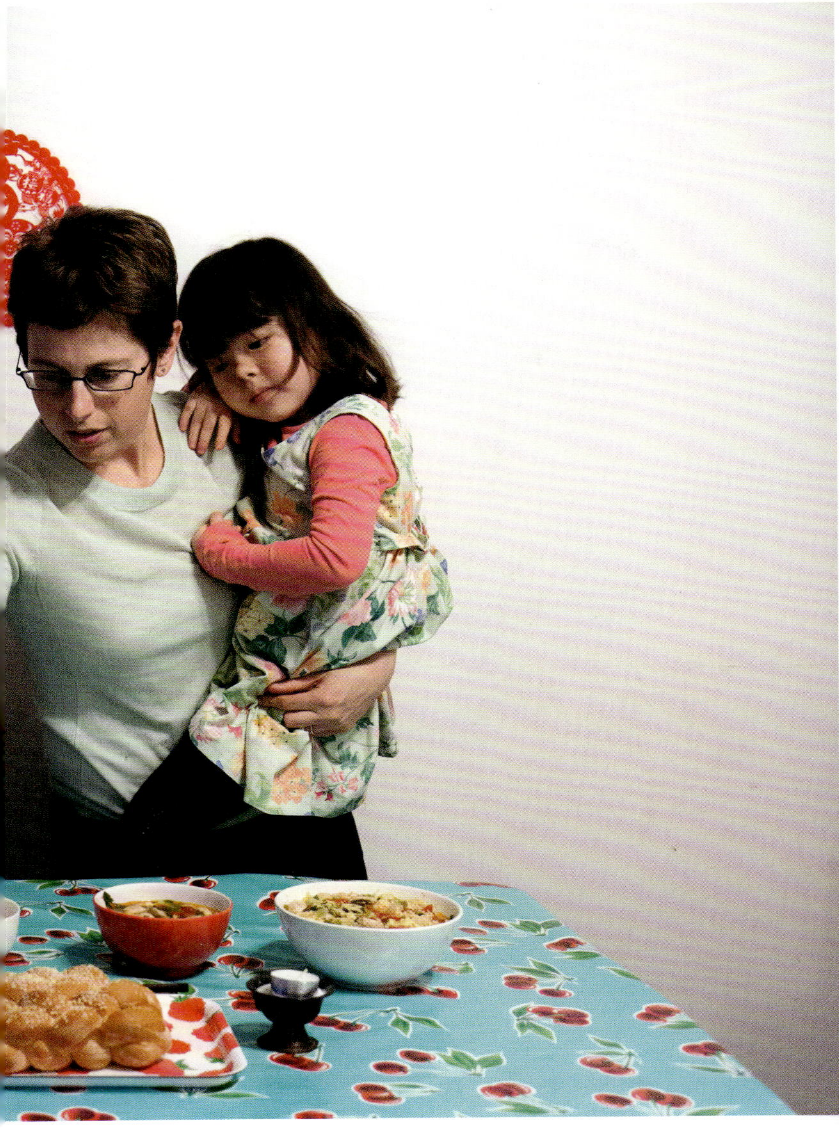

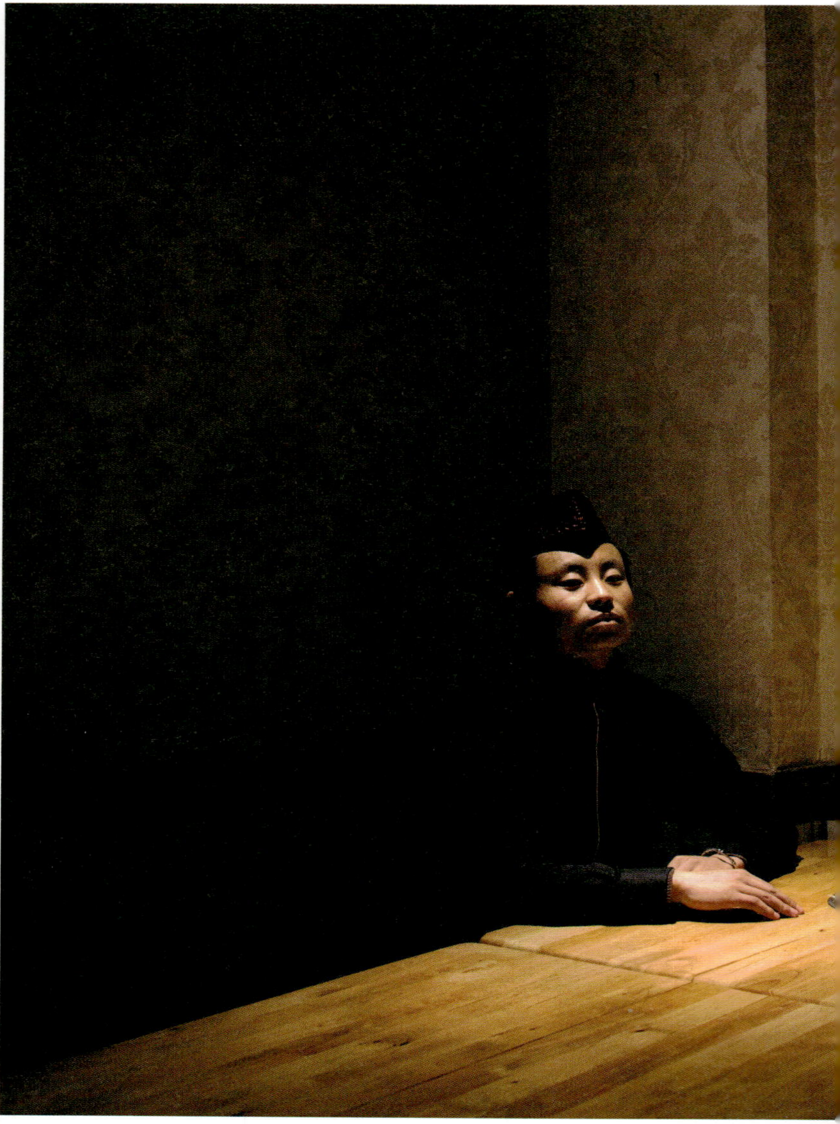

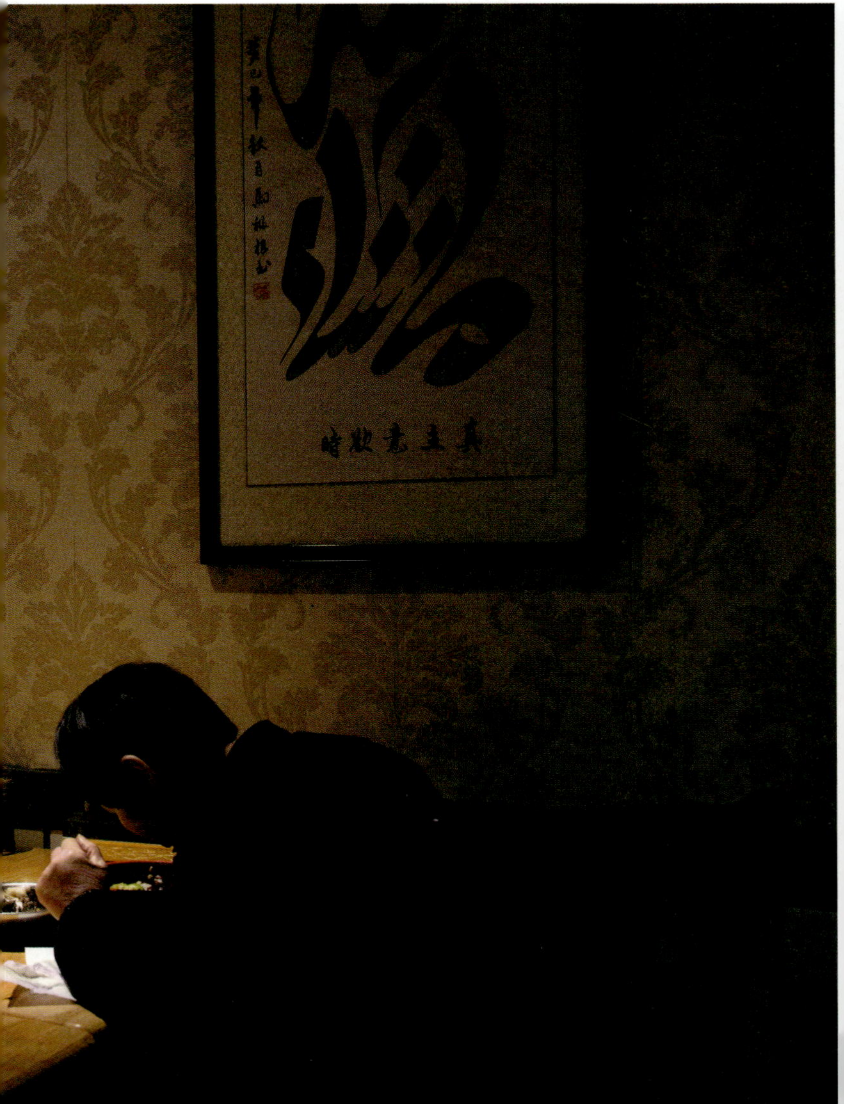

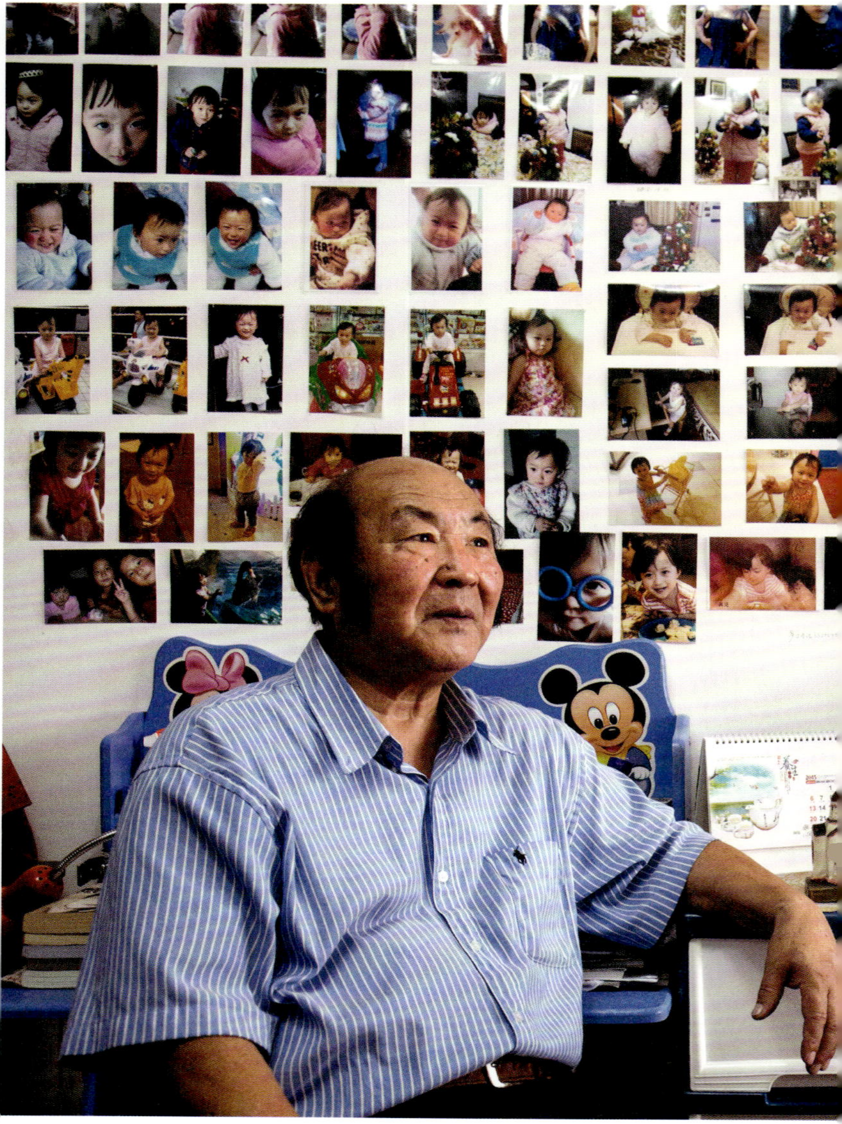

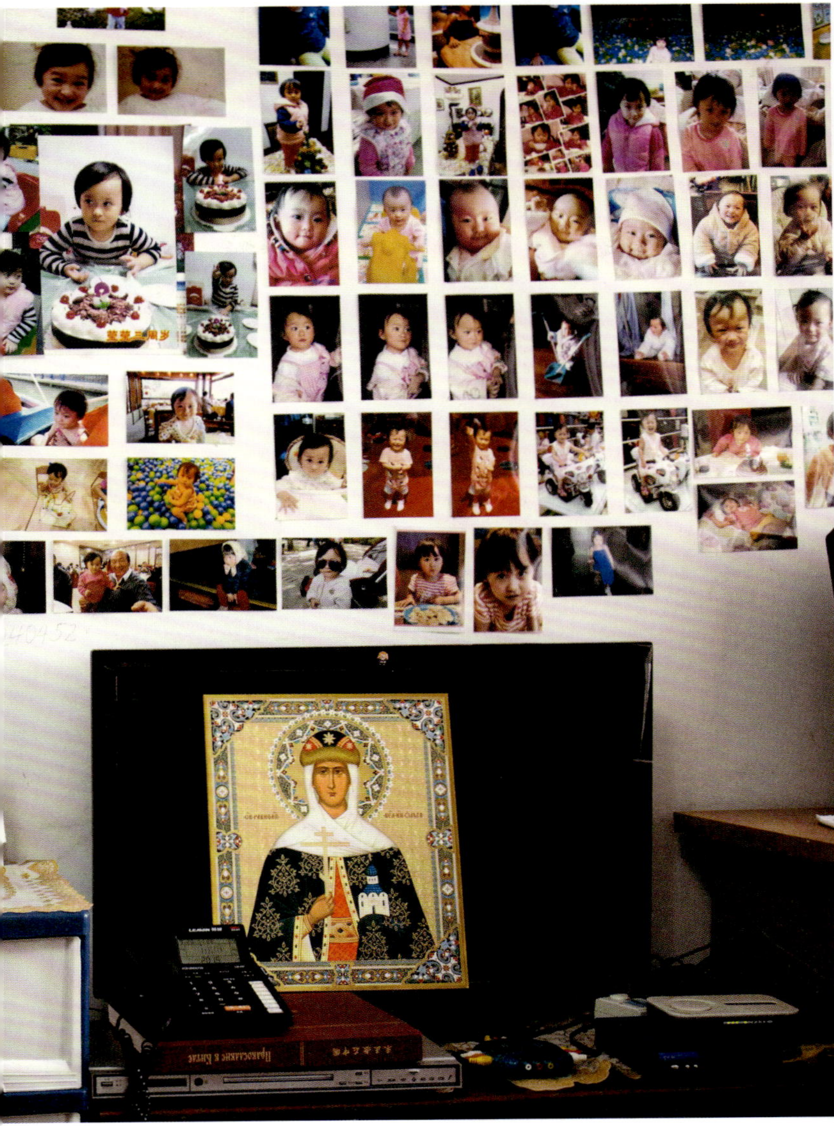
Православие в Китае

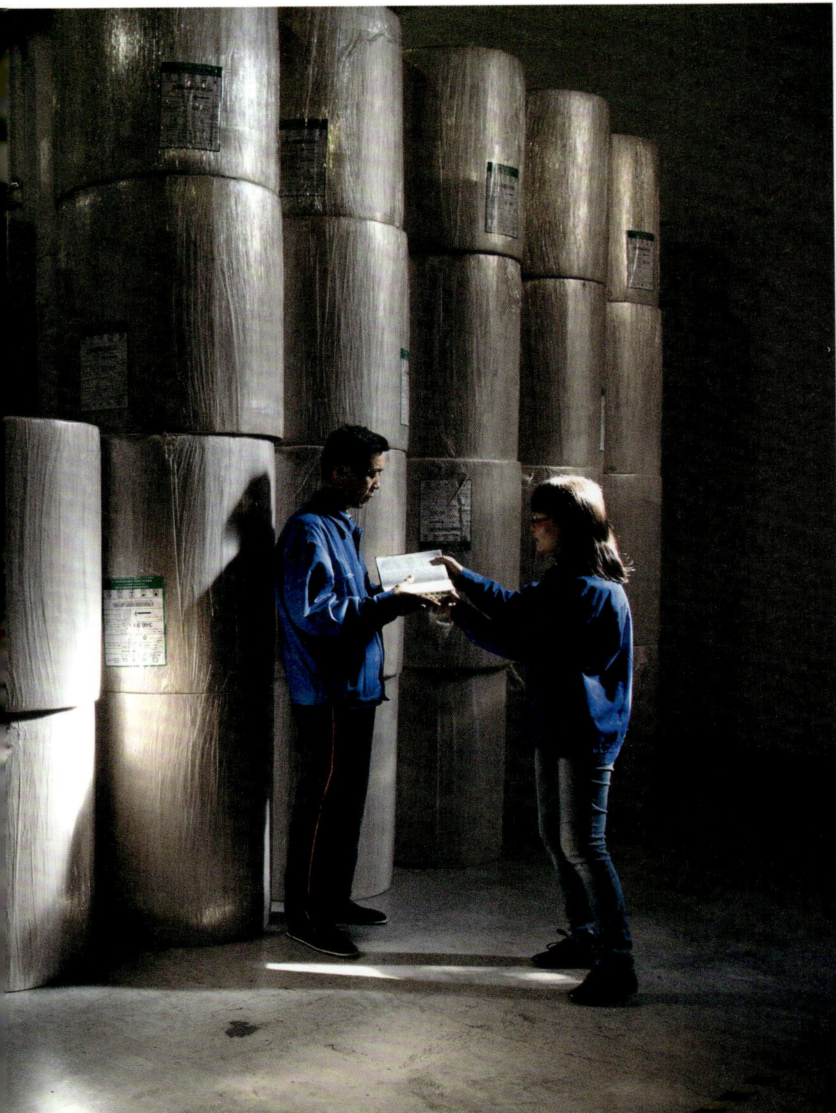

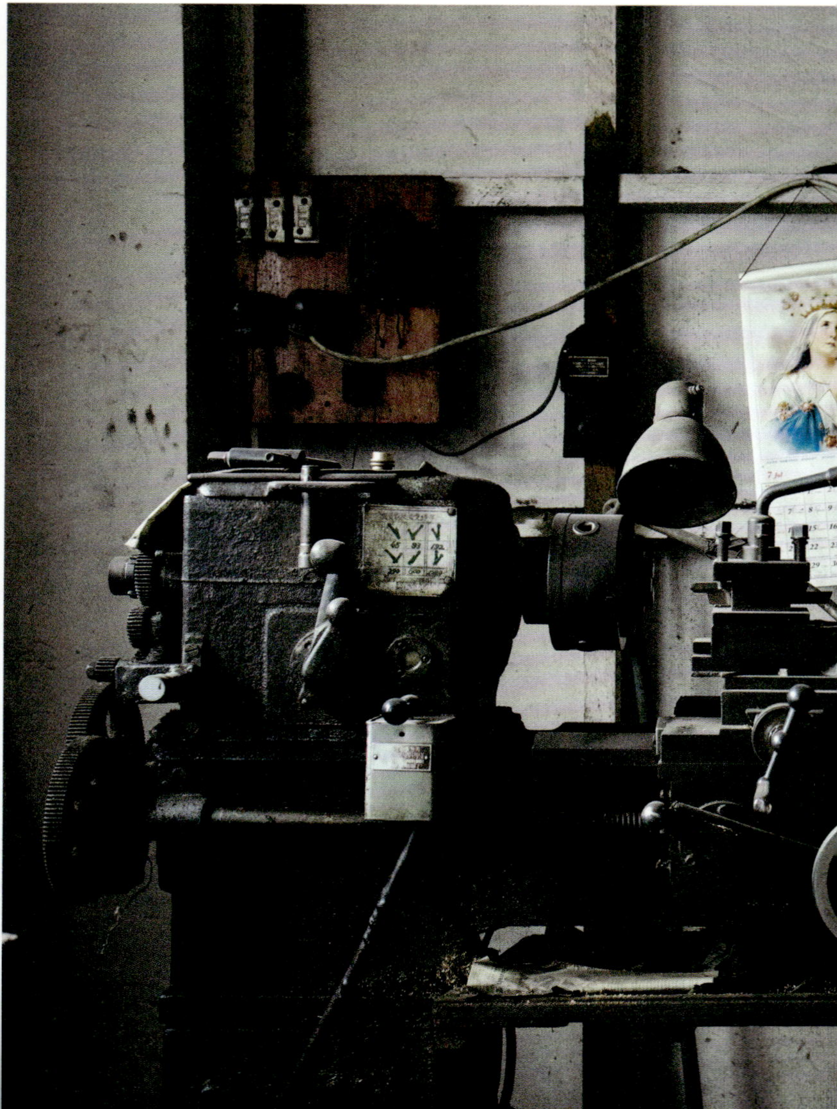

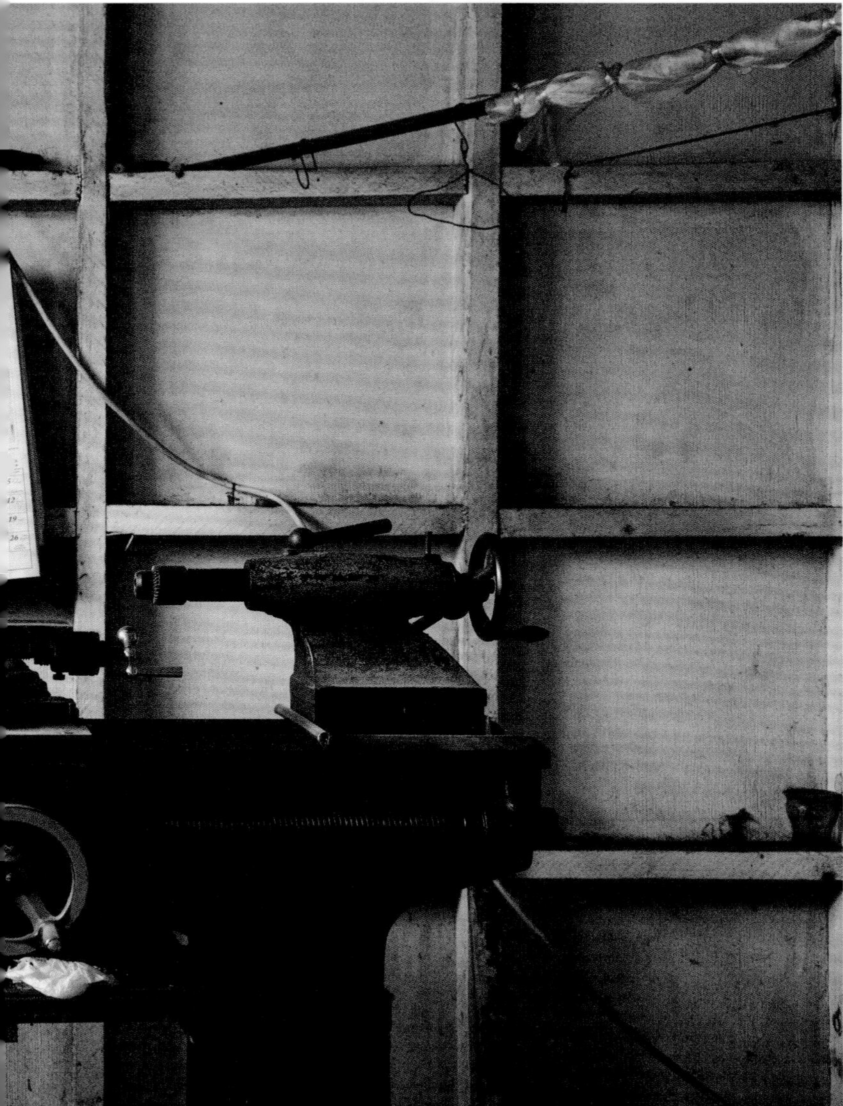

49

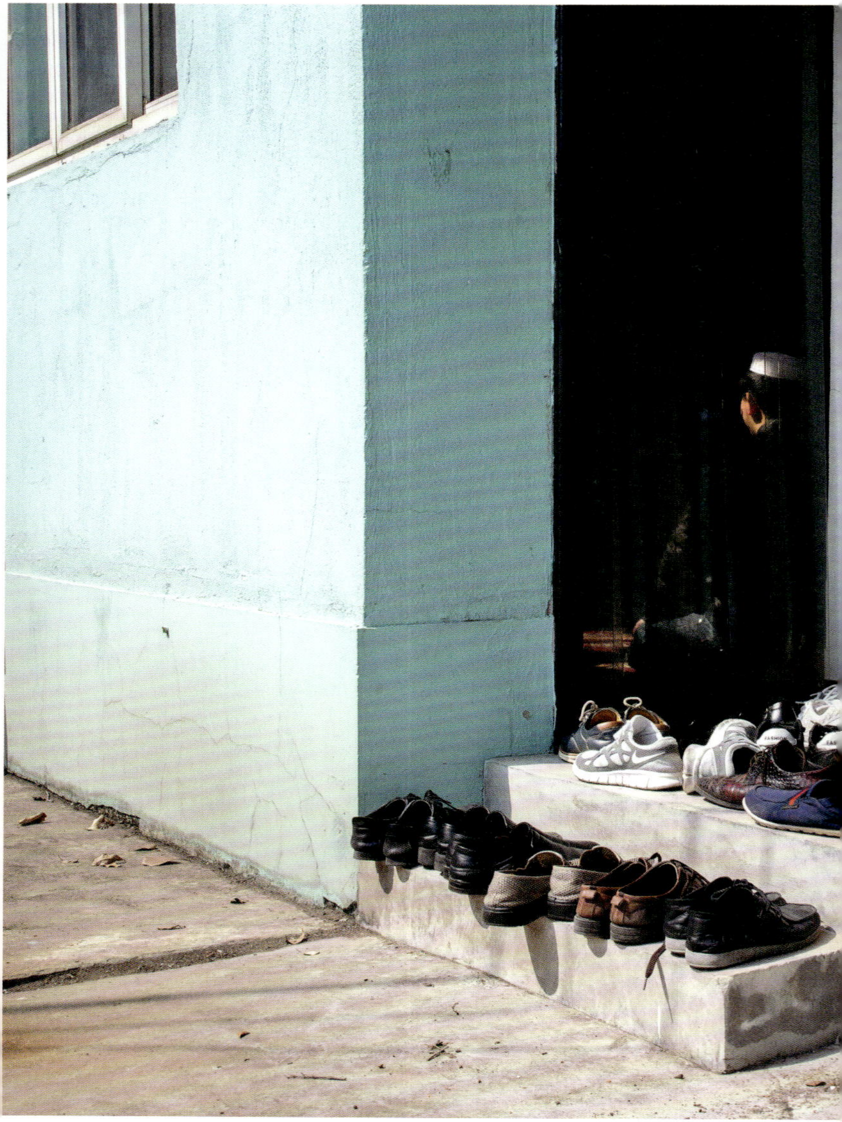

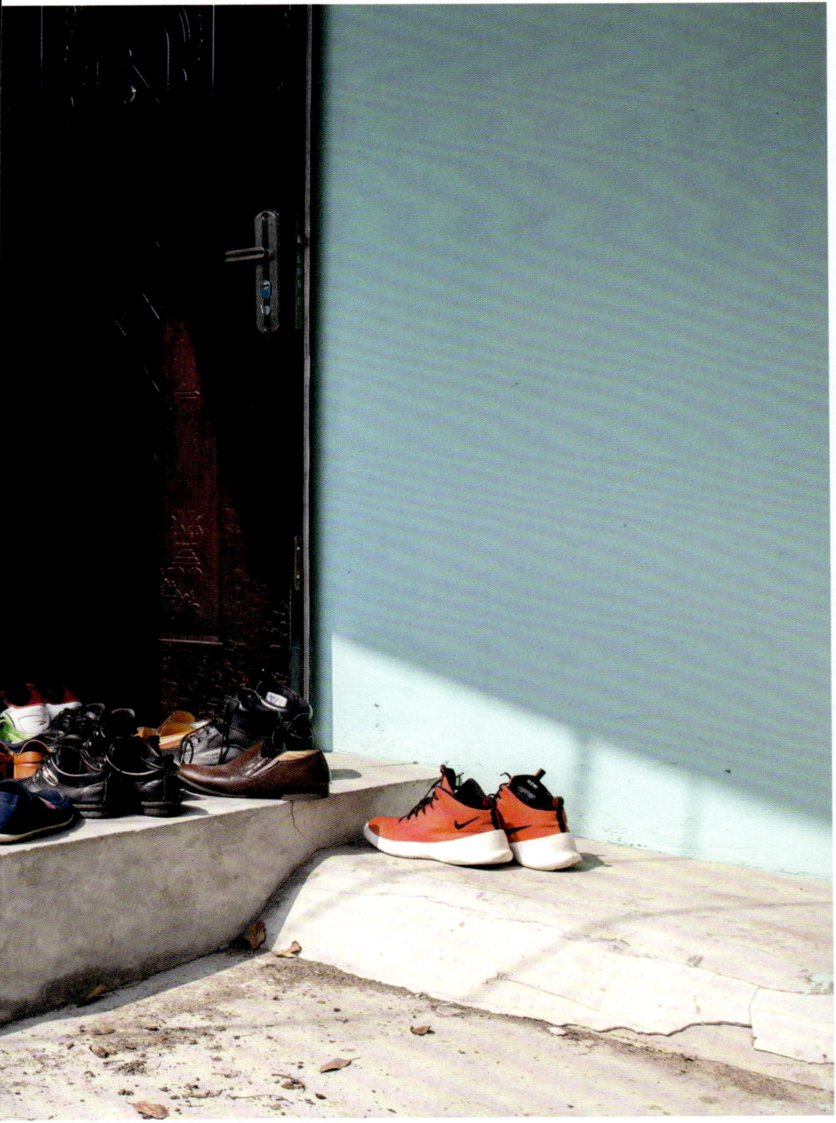

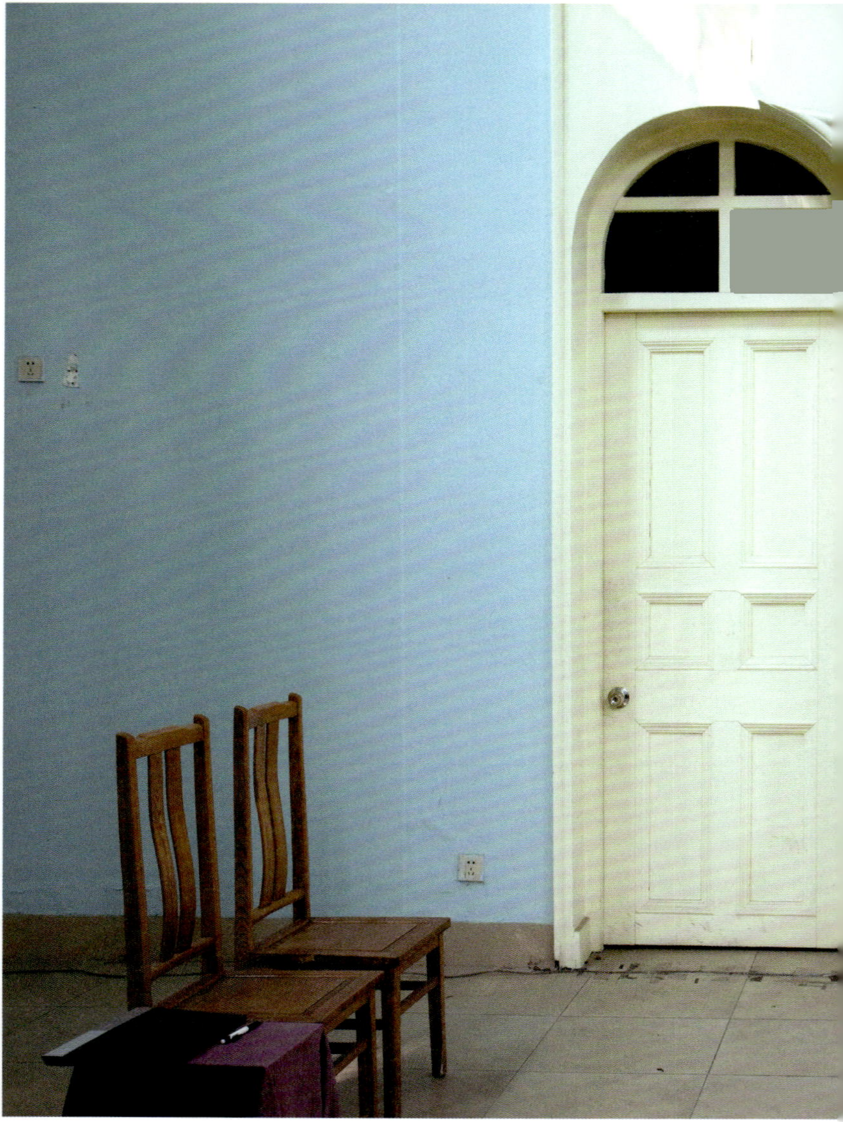

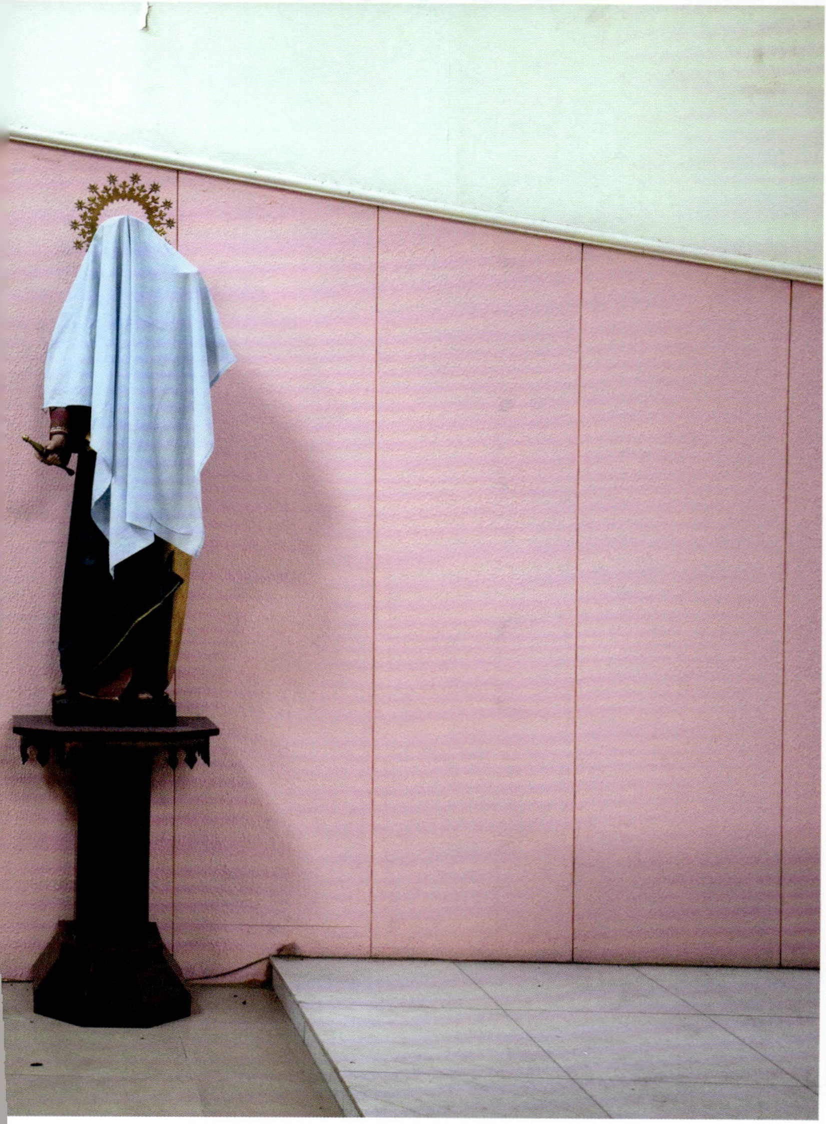

Sacred Shanghai
First published in 2019 by
GOST Books
8a West Smithfield
London, EC1A 9JR
info@gostbooks.com
gostbooks.com

Designed and produced by GOST:
Katie Clifford, Gemma Gerhard, Justine Hucker, Allon Kaye, Eleanor Macnair, Claudia Paladini, Ana Rocha

Printed in Italy by Conti Tipocolor

British Library cataloguing-in-publication data. A catalogue record of this book is available from the British Library.

ISBN 978-1-910401-38-5